THE Business OF Audio Engineering

About the Cover

The cover photo represents for me one of the most profound developments in the evolution of recording equipment. For years SSL has led the way in large-format recording consoles. They saw the change in the industry and stepped out to meet the need.

The development of the AWS-900 more than any other product now allows the ultimate professional recording experience to exist anywhere. When you think about audio recording as a career at this time, you now have more options than ever before. Literally every area of the content building world has an audio component attached. Just like SSL we all need to look ahead for the needs of our industry and be willing to step forward to craft new ways to create better content.

THE Business OF
Audio Engineering

By Dave Hampton

HAL•LEONARD®

Hal Leonard Books
An Imprint of Hal Leonard Corporation
New York

Published in 2008 by Hal Leonard Books
An Imprint of Hal Leonard Corporation
7777 West Bluemound Road
Milwaukee, WI 53213

Trade Book Division Editorial Offices
19 West 21st Street, New York, NY 10010

Printed in the United States of America

Cover and book design by Stephen Ramirez
Cover photo courtesy of Solid State Logic

Library of Congress Cataloging-in-Publication Data is available upon request.

ISBN 978-1-4234-5400-7

www.halleonard.com

To my wife Lisa, without whom I would have never started writing. By the time this hits the shelves, we will have a new daughter. I am so excited. Thanks for making my home life loving and filled with laughter. We have much to do! I love you.

FOR MY FATHER AND MOTHER

Thanks for the Gifts

I am forty-six years old. My son is twenty-one, my daughter is eighteen and my wife and I have a newborn on the way. Doing this book while waiting to become a parent again has caused me to think about my mom and dad a lot and the sacrifices they made to give my brother and me whatever advantages they could.

My father's name was Kenneth Robert Hampton. He passed away when I was nineteen years old. He was an accountant by profession, but he was also an avid record collector. I can remember listening to jazz records as I did my list of chores each weekend. Years after my dad's passing, my mom explained to me that while my dad had a career as an accountant, he only did it because it could pay a good wage and allow him to provide for his family. He really did not like it at all. His real love was music. He was so dedicated to his family's survival that he did a job he didn't enjoy. In fact, he did that job so well that he became the first African American accountant that Desilu Studios (Desi Arnez and Lucille Ball) had in the 1960s.

I always think about my dad because of the people that my career has brought me into contact with, especially jazz musicians. I know he would have been proud. I feel that the music he played while my brother and I did chores was his investment in my career. While he never lived to experience any of my career highlights, his grandchildren, or daughter-in-law, I do believe that his manner and his way of being was imprinted on me as a child. Audio achievements are cool, but being a husband and father is the number one calling for my life.

My mom is still alive and has always been my biggest fan. She gave me her New York City street smarts. She has been a nurse for over fifty years. I was always amazed at how my mom switched easily from nurse to mother, from speaking Spanish to speaking English. She is a brilliant woman. My mom's skill set is so big it throws people off because she only stands 4' 11". I think she was the first person to ever show me how to actively turn prejudice and discrimination into positive energy. When I think of the skills that helped me in life as well as my career, I am brought right back to the lessons from Mom and Dad.

I know there are others like me whose parents were the first generation to come up after the depression. Undoubtedly they have heard them say, "What you need is a good job with good benefits." Always remember, not everyone has the drive and the calling to be an entrepreneur, independent contractor, or their own boss. I do it because it is my passion and because I knew early on that I would be doing exactly what I am doing. I enjoy using my gifts to help as many people and situations as possible. My advice to anyone who has what they feel is a passion for their chosen profession is to think for a moment about your childhood and what experiences you had that possibly led you to where you are today. You will find that your career chose you, just as much as you chose your career.

CONTENTS

Contents

FOREWORD

Throughout most of the history of the audio industry, people learned the craft of audio engineering through the apprenticeship system. They got a job (any job!) in a recording studio and worked their way up to assistant engineer, and then to first engineer. Occasionally, the process was swift, but most often the path took years of watching, listening and learning from others along with much trial and error. However, in recent years with the proliferation of schools that offer programs in audio, large numbers of graduates from those programs have entered the work force without the benefits of on-the-job training. Add to that fact the reality that many of those who pursue work in the audio industry are, by nature, more interested in the creative and technical areas than the business aspects of the industry. The result is that there are now a lot of people working—or trying to get work—in the audio field with little real-world training and even less business experience.

Enter Dave Hampton. Dave has spent many years accumulating not only technical knowledge, but also business and people skills, and he commands the respect of both his peers and the artists he works with. In this book, as in his previous book, *So You're an Audio Engineer . . .*, Dave combines his natural sense of what's right and fair with his life and work experience to offer both a unique perspective on the industry and some very solid advice. He shares stories from his career and shows us that, in a changing world and a changing industry, the qualities of honesty, integrity and respect for others really do still matter, and that there's no substitute for experience and hard work. Dave's love of the recording process and the recording business itself shines throughout his words, and anyone who reads them will benefit from his thoughts on how to succeed.

Maureen Droney,
Author, *Mixmasters: Platinum Engineers Share Their Secrets for Success*

INTRODUCTION

Why This Book Right Now?
A Note From the Author

Well, that is easy. Right now we have an industry that is in full evolution. Technology and time have now allowed many people to participate in the full range of arts-related activity. Structured education has now positioned itself to certify any and all who have the entrance fee. With everyone running the fast track to live the dream of getting paid from his or her beats, breaks, songs, lyrics, raps, and ring tones, no one has stopped to think about how to successfully navigate and handle the business on business terms. For the audio engineer it is one thing to be able to work Pro Tools quicker than anyone in the room. It is a whole different set of skills needed to work consistently and be able to make money beyond the normal work-for-hire exchange.

With all the books teaching us how to mix, no one has ever given us relevant information on what to charge or how to take all this newfound audio school education training and earn a living. We all read the magazines and see the same recognizable faces of successful engineering presented. Well, so what? It is about what you do right now that will make a difference in your career.

The stories and examples I give are from interviews with many successful working engineers as well as experiences from my own career. What I am offering to you in this book are some ideas and strategies that we all have discovered about ourselves as independent engineers, and the community of creative artists and situations we all serve. Please use the hard data in this book to assist you in being proactive about your professional journey. I personally believe that we are all in this together, both the engineer that has thirty years as well as the engineer with three months experience. It is a skilled craft and it must always be respected. Consider this book as an opportunity to counsel with others who have come before you.

I looked at all the books that are considered mandatory reading for anyone seeking a career in the recording industry. None of them spent more than a precious few pages when it came to the discussion of recording as a process, let alone the topic of engineers, compensation, etc. While one had a line item figure on a sample invoice, all of them saw this role as nothing more than that of a minor player.

Imagine that; an entire profession reduced to a line item entry. Not everyone wants to be an artist. It is because of this systematic devaluation of the importance of our profession that I chose to spend time gathering information and sharing stories that show how to work consistently and prosper, and how to recognize all kinds of business signs and situations. The stories that I share from personal experiences are 100 percent true. The names have been left out to protect the ignorant. Have fun reading this and get your pen out because some of this goes way beyond engineering!

1

Education and Training

THE GUIDANCE COUNSELOR IS NOT ALWAYS RIGHT

We will begin in high school because it was a huge turning point in my life. My parents did their best to ensure that both my older brother and I did not fall the way of most kids in our neighborhood. My dad was an accountant and my mom was a registered nurse. The climate in our South Central Los Angeles neighborhood was similar to the rawness of the Wild West. The Crips and Bloods (notorious L.A. gangs) were being born just blocks away. So my parents sent us to a local private school right in the middle of the 'hood. Walter A. Meyer Memorial High School was known to all as the "Lutheran High School."

It was 1978, and I was a junior getting ready for the first meeting with my guidance counselor. I always remember that time because as anyone who is the younger sibling of an upperclassman can tell you, meetings like that are one-on-one. You actually look forward to going because it makes you feel like you are beginning to grow up. My guidance counselor was the same guy who had also met with my brother several years earlier. So he figured he knew me because he knew my brother.

As we met, he informed me that, by looking at my grades and test scores, he thought that I would be better off in the military. He said I should not think about college because my test scores showed no aptitude for being able to "hang" at the college level. I listened and was very polite—a long-time Hampton trait. I thanked him, got up, and went back to class. I said nothing to my friends. I began to look around, trying to blend in because I really started to feel stupid.

When I went home that day, the scene kept replaying in my mind. I spoke to my mom very little when she asked me about the meeting. I just tried to make it through until the weekend.

For fun on the weekends my friends and I would DJ—spin records at parties and dances. I liked building the wooden stands for the light and sound equipment. I remember going to hook up some gear once and my friend said to me, "Don't touch that shit man, you don't know nothing about how it works. You don't have a technical brain." I said okay and began to link that statement with the guidance counselor's remarks earlier that week.

Then I got angry.

As I left my friend's house that day, I made a vow in my head to learn "that shit" better than anyone else. Day and night I worked with the gear, the records, and the lights. I learned all of it and ended up buying my friend out and doing it by myself for a little while. Being a DJ let me have a separate persona so that I could forget about all the negative things that people liked to say. Being able to DJ a party well was a way to use my ears, hands, and feelings to give me the strength to see my true reality, and not my guidance counselor's or friend's negative perceptions.

Being a DJ also taught me how to read an audience, how music can control the pace of an event, and how to use my mind to concentrate on two separate things at once. I learned so much from that time in my life, including several key things about myself as well:

1. Other people's words are not my reality.

2. I will define what I can and cannot do.

3. God only made one me, so already I am the best.

Since that time I have noticed a pattern in my life. I have always been motivated partly by the negative input of others. I seem to use problems, setbacks, and situations as gasoline to help me power through and get results. My ambition is also a big plus, as many of my greatest successes in this business have come from accepting unwanted projects that others had avoided.

And just for the sake of accuracy and the guidance counselor's peace of mind, my brother was the one who went into the military and gave twenty years of distinguished service before retiring.

FORMAL EDUCATION

I went to Los Angeles Trade Tech College for electronics, as well as California State, Dominguez Hills for Electronic Music and Recording. My technical capabilities—being able to not only run a recording session, but also fix anything that broke down during it—gave me a huge advantage over the guys just studying music.

Initially I entered school to learn audio engineering. While in school, I was able to work as an engineer for a radio syndication house where I recorded radio shows and commercials, as well as Armed Forces Radio and other album work. I saw early on that the road of engineering is paved with a lot of sessions that are not as interesting as others. I also saw that I could use my technical skills to get on the road. Once I was on the job as a technician, if the skills needed were that of an engineer, I had that to offer as well.

Working while still in school let me see and experience the real world of engineering (this was way before Pro Tools). By the time my career was under way, I had a wealth of experience and credits to boot, so I decided to keep the engineering second to the technical so I would stand out and so that I could not be denied participation due to lack of knowledge.

I began work at Oberheim Electronics once I finished school, which was an invaluable experience—the foundation that I built there is still with me today. I credit Pete Munsen and Tom Dunn for giving me the knowledge of troubleshooting as well as my full understanding of analog synthesizer technology and circuit design. Those two techs from Minnesota shared all they knew with a kid fresh out of school. I loved my job, and received knowledge about computers that others did not consider important yet. (It may be hard to picture a studio without a computer now, but then computers had not fully entered music production.)

My workday at Oberheim started at 7:30 a.m. and ended at about 3:30 p.m.. I was a bench technician and an audio tester for drum machines and synthesizers, as well as a tradeshow representative and artist relations contact. Not long after I got the Oberheim gig, I started doing free-lance technician work in commercial and private studios after I left my day job. Sometimes I would work from about 4:00 p.m. to 12:00 midnight. I was getting a real education in the music business! I was also making more money in two or three days of freelance technician work than I did at the regular gig in an entire week.

In my freelance work I did everything from transport and setup of Synclaviers ($150,000 music production system), custom keyboard and drum machine modifications, programming drum sounds on chips, and on-site repair while sessions were going on. If anything that made a sound was broken, I fixed it. If a way to do something did not exist, I figured it out as best I could to make the clients happy. I had no shame because the name of the game was *work*.

Even though I knew all the electronics that I did, I also knew I had to figure out a way to be in the room. I learned how to transport and set up large keyboard systems because I knew no one would go to the degree that I would. I realized that the hip stuff was going on *inside* the studio, and I needed to be in there! I used technician work as my "Trojan Horse" to get me into the sessions.

And it worked very well. A lot of keyboard players that I worked with used my set-up service because I did the job with pride and always made the client look their best even before they were in the room.

I always remember the phrase, "I'm just trying to get my foot in the door." Just make sure the door that your foot is in does not lead to the broom closet!

2

Building Confidence

BE SATISFIED WITH A JOB WELL DONE

Over the years I think I have consulted and built at least thirty-five studios. I came into the industry at a time when the home studio community was just starting. If you're wondering why home studios took off, let's look at the math: If an artist takes $50,000 and builds his own studio, then directs all his recording projects toward his own studio, that would mean that the monies going to the studio now go the artist/owner. If an album budget was $150,000, then he or she (artist/studio owner) made his/her original $50,000 back and can get a large portion of the $100,000 that remains.

This is a simplified explanation of the mentality that was in place when the home studio started to take over. I have seen all levels of artists do the home studio thing. In all those years, I have had only a handful of people who have actually come to me and say, "Thanks."

I remember doing a remote recording in 2002 in Hollywood. I was going from the truck to the stage and I happened to see a recording artist for whom I had built a large home production studio in Sacramento several years earlier. I said, "Hello," and we began talking about old times. As we finished and exchanged office information, he said to me, "Never got a chance to thank you man."

I said, "For what?"

He said, "Man, I made so much money in that studio! I wrote so many songs!"

In all my years of doing work for hire, I had never heard someone say those words. At that instant, I knew that my participation in the small studio world was definitely meant to be. The home studio as it was then has drastically changed. The mindset is still the same today; however, the budgets have gone way down.

I share this story of thanks to simply say that I did my work because I wanted to make a difference, and at the end of the day, I wanted my clients to be satisfied with a job well done.

I designed and built recording rooms and large studios at a time when there was no one who looked like me doing it. My methods were homegrown, but they worked, and people liked the results.

Part of being satisfied with a job well done is being satisfied with yourself and your skills. I remember when I did a consultation on a studio design and ended up screwing myself royally because I was not satisfied with who I was. I did a consultation for a church down south. I was actually in town to work with one artist, and got the new gig while I was there.

Up to that point, I did all my big rooms the same way as the small rooms—I made the drawings, the model, and then I hired the crew and oversaw the work. Design fees are great things when you are a one-man gang like me, but I wanted to grow, so I said to myself, "I'll hire a local architectural firm to do some of the initial drawings and design model! It will look professional." *Wrong!*

I hunted and found what was said to be one of the top firms in town. Now realize, in my mind I was spending money to make money. I figured that I would work with the firm to get the design and presentation model done and be weeks ahead of schedule. Well, several weeks and several thousands of dollars later, I was hit with the cold hard truth.

1. There was nothing wrong with how I did my designs before.

2. When you involve others, you risk being a slave to their schedule.

By our second meeting, the guys did not have what I needed, nor did they produce any of my hand-drawn sketches or notes. They just took my money and had no intention of meeting my deadline. I explained what had happened with the architects to my client. I showed the client what I had already paid out and then returned all of the money that was left from my deposit. I also went after the architectural firm for breach of contract.

I did not even try to salvage that potential job. In my effort to appear what I thought was more "professional," I had lost too much time and money to do the job well. I share that story to say, "Be satisfied within yourself, know who you are, and remember that the same skills that got you to the game keep you in the game."

Every time I do what I do successfully, I look at it as a direct slam-dunk in the face of anyone who said I (or anyone like me) could not do that kind of work. The opportunity to work should be extended to all, not just a select few. If they gave royalties to studio designers for studios that produced hits, then I—and several other not-so-well-known studio guys—would be rich!

The payoff for me is the fact that when someone works in a room that I have built, large or small, I get the satisfaction of knowing that the concept to create the space they work in came from my head. That is why when I get a project, I consider each job special. All jobs look impossible to those who never try.

I actually believe that many large designers will start to look at the home studio/small room market differently. They may even try to tailor products specifically for them. For years I have always thought that the strength of the retail industry was in the home recording market. When I started doing home studios I used to say, "Little money is money too."

The home studio boom did a lot for the industry. The main thing I saw was that hit records recorded in home studios did a lot to dispel the stories record executives would tell artists. They told them what they had to do, where they had to work, and that there was nothing that they (as an artist) could do about how the record company allocated the budget money for their record.

Furthermore, it gave the young engineers on some of those recordings a chance to have careers. The guys who cut the first hit records in home studios were trying to do their best work in supposedly less than professional settings. At the end of the day, they too were satisfied with a job well done.

3

Professionalism

I call this next story "Less Than Half." It comes directly to you from one of my most famous clients. He and I have known each other since we both started in the business. When we met many years ago he was the opening act and I was the technician underneath the stage with a computer rig, keyboards, and a TV screen playing back vocal samples for the headliner. He would come visit me underneath after each show and say, "Hey, man, what are you doing?" We would talk for hours about technology and computers.

Over the years we stayed in touch and I did some minor technical work for him. About ten years ago we were eating lunch when he said, "Dave I have a space and I want to build a studio there. Can you help me?" I said okay. He gave me the dimensions and I sketched out a plan for a creative space in the area he said was available. Well, ten years later he stumbled across the drawings and said, "Hey man, I'm ready to build that spot!"

I was surprised that he still had the drawings. In the ten years that had passed, we had both done well. My concern was our friendship first and the project second. We decided that I would do the labor at a fixed price and the time for the job would flex around both of our schedules. He would basically pay for materials and the crew's time. And I charged him a minor fee for using my design. This way he could spend the majority of his budget on the studio equipment. To help him even more, I would connect him to all the suppliers that I use. That way he could directly negotiate his deals for equipment. By doing these things I knew the studio would be up and running in no time flat, and our friendship would be intact.

It only took five weeks and it was done. As he started looking for gear at a music store one day he was confronted by a guy who said, "I hear you are building a studio. I could have done it for less than half of what it cost!"

He looked at him and laughed and said, "You don't even know what I paid!"

The guy realized that his obvious attempt to put himself in a good standing had backfired. He chuckled and said, "I know man. I just need some work."

Think the story ends there? It does not! My friend went equipment shopping another day and two other guys approach him and said, "Man watch that Dave Hampton guy because he will overcharge you for equipment!"

My client let them go on. Then he said, "Have you guys ever worked with Dave Hampton?"

"Well, no."

"Do you even know Dave Hampton?"

"No, but that's what we heard."

"Well, we should call him right now so you can talk with him and find out!" he said. The guy was speechless. Nonetheless, my friend didn't buy anything from them.

They did not know the truth about the situation. They just saw a famous person and thought by smearing me they could get him to do business with them. To smear others, only smears you. My friend called me and told me about it, and I started to get angry. My friend stopped me and said, "Man you are doing something right if you have all these people talking about you!" He also went on to share with me that as his popularity grew so did his list of detractors. I have heard this from many other famous clients as well. They all tell me the same thing: do not worry about folks that do not like you.

Here is the truth straight from my mouth: I have not sold gear to clients for over fifteen years! When I started doing larger jobs it became more important for me to concentrate on getting the facilities finished on time, on budget, running well, and looking good. I would direct the clients to retailers and not even take finder's fees or other normal cash incentives.

The reason I still do that is because taking kickbacks can cause you to appear more focused on making kickbacks than on making a great project come to life. In my view, the client already pays me for advice to benefit them. If the advice I give is based on anything other than the truth, it would make my advice and me look suspect. So, along with doing my work, I leave no room for negative input.

Any successful person knows that the letters CYA stands for "cover your ass." Ours is a service business, so at the end of each day as long as you pay my wage, I will honor our work together. All I ask is that you spell my name correctly on the check.

When I work a job for any of my clients, confidentiality is number one. When I did the re-design of Paisley Park for Prince it was after every other studio designer had been there and told him what was wrong, or that it would never work properly. I got the job because I let him tell me what was wrong and we worked to make what he wanted possible.

The success we had was due in part to the fact that I worked in secret for one year. By the time anyone knew I was doing any work for him, I was done with the major problem areas. None of the experts had time to even render a comment. In the end, Prince is still making and selling records and all those experts who said that the studio would never work correctly were wrong.

Despite my efforts to always be the most helpful to my clients, I still garner disrespect, hate, and jealousy from others. The way I look at it is this: I have been in this business consistently contributing for over twenty-five years. I am far too busy being myself to be concerned about anyone who thinks that by speaking badly about me they can create a road to work. That is not the way to create solid business relationships. Haters will always be there, so do not lose time worrying about whether or not they love you!

Just like the first guy whose comment was "I could have done it for less than half," all the antagonists described above have one thing in common. They all give less than half an effort. You get out of your career what you put into it.

If you are looking at engineering as a career, do everyone some good and learn your craft while developing a close relationship with the truth. This will help you develop good strong business relationships that give you results. Your dollars are directly related to your productivity; not to your ability to talk about others or try to get work from others through negative means.

In addition to the suggestions above, always be mindful of who you are as an engineer on a project. As an audio engineer you will be asked to work with not only music industry folks, but also video editors, directors, and advertising people. Content takes many forms. Audio is just one aspect of some of these projects. Knowing who you are in a project helps you define your success and play the correct support role. On projects where you are the creator of the content, it helps you give better direction to others who are supporting you.

The tricks and tips that many refuse to share all come from adapting skill sets. Some engineers, new and old, do not want to share anything because they feel it would give others an advantage. However, I as well as some other engineer friends would not be here if it were not for two types of engineers who influenced us:

TYPE 1: The engineers who shared, let us look, and gave us a shot.

TYPE 2: The engineers who would not share, said no, and snubbed us.

Here are some tips and information from Type 1 that will help you and your work stand out:

Do not wait until you have a chance to work with someone before you start exploring your creative options. Use your down time to know your tools better.

Document and begin keeping a notebook of your ideas and observations. Pay attention to detail.

When I started, I did all types of recording. I had to keep notebooks to keep all the project delivery requirements straight. If I was doing a show like Armed Forces Radio, I would need several tones at the top of the tape that had to be exactly in the same place every time. If I was doing a radio spot, I only needed one tone at the top and sometimes a countdown.

Keeping all this in my head while trying to engineer or assist every chance was challenging enough. Notes help you keep your facts straight. When I started working with individual producers I kept notes on every aspect of what I observed when they were in session. Eventually my tenacity was rewarded by being asked to work in their pre-production sessions too.

Do your homework and research how things were done to achieve certain sounds on records. When you begin to work with clients, try to gather details about how they process musical thought.

What music do they like? What writing style do they have? Do they understand formal composition? Do they play an instrument?

This information is crucial when beginning to work with someone. As an engineer, having this information can assist you in helping your clients get the best out of themselves and out of the situation they are experiencing with you. Many engineers do this through conversation and just being themselves. They find that getting to know someone (no matter how brief the time) helps to create the proper vibe in the room.

Always try to be on time. A call beats no call. Time is money. Do I need to keep going? In this day of cell phones and e-mails there is no excuse for not staying in communication. When you are part of a team, especially in the role of engineer, you can affect everyone involved by not calling or notifying other team members about schedule changes.

Pay attention to how you look. I am fully supportive of creative expression. However, as an engineer, unless this helps you mix better, pay close attention to how you look when you are going to work with others. Many young interns let their dress reflect their desire to stand out and be noticed, rather than dressing for the role of assistant or intern. I am the first one to speak out against discrimination of any kind, but let's be real for a minute, dress like crap and you will not be asked back. Remember you are selling yourself, and if you are interviewing for a staff position in a corporate setting you will potentially be representing the company. Dressing to fit the setting shows professionalism and consideration for the business at hand.

Keep your personal problems to yourself. There is no time for special stories and excuses when you are breaking into this business. Many experienced engineers have had several long relationships and marriages go down because of the time and commitment required by session life. While I do not suggest it, I can speak from experience. Problems for me were a great way to challenge myself to focus at work. I found when my relationship was off my skill set was really on. It took years for me to understand how to create balance in my life. In addition, try to keep your personal unmet needs out of your work setting. There is nothing more uncomfortable than seeing someone so in need financially that every opportunity to work becomes a mini drama of epic proportions.

Create balance in your life. Read books and spend time away from the isolated recording experience. Spend time with family and friends. Go fishing, hiking, or golfing. Whatever you choose, know that after about six to seven hours in the studio your hearing and attention to detail takes a dip. Rest your ears. Take some time to work on the most important thing . . . your life!

Experiment. There is no wrong way. I often laugh at some engineers who are privileged enough to have lots of gear and lots of work. They constantly try to imply that their way is "the" way because they have done the research. While I applaud them for using their privileged status and opportunity to do precious research, I cannot support their obvious pompous nature when sharing their data. Many hit songs were born from poorly financed recording sessions in less-than-adequate studios.

Even if someone tells you what he or she did, take the time to do it yourself. If you do not have a Pro Tools HD rig, do it on your LE rig but do it so you can train your ears to understand the nuances of a DAW creative lifestyle. Learn several different software programs. While Pro Tools is an accepted standard, Logic and Digital Performer also play roles in many creative settings. Use the gear that you have access to and challenge yourself to simulate the conditions. When you eliminate all the choices, you go back to recording as it began—when microphone placement was king.

I remember when DATs first came out and we had a bunch of people speculating about how hard to drive the input. At that time the Panasonic 3700 was the DAT of choice in the studio, but the Sony machine was the choice in all the A&R offices. Listening back and reference mixing to the Sony machine as opposed to the 3700 at least let you know what your mixes would sound like when they got to the label.

I still hear the same conversation today when it comes to burning CDs. Well, what are you waiting for? Do it yourself! On a side note, take the time to find out who your reference materials go to for review when you are dealing with record companies and artist-driven situations. Try to know the people in the process from A&R to mastering.

Stay current on technology. Read trade magazines, monitor websites for software update information. Learn the most popular brand of DAWs being used by potential clients.

Learning new information always gives you the edge. Combine that with even an intern position and you have the makings of an opportunity. Many engineers started out by knowing a simple piece of information at a critical time when they were interns.

Keep everything relevant to the project you are working on. It really is important that you focus on what you are doing. Outside input is great but the only thing that makes what you do belong to you is the fact that YOU do it. Many other people can have experience that outshines yours but the fact is, it is your client now so that means it is your time to do what you feel is best for the job you are on. Being right by the book standard sometimes is not the right thing to do. I have seen many engineers answer questions in such a way as to remain blameless rather than answer directly. Stand up for your bad choices as well as the good ones; it shows responsibility.

It ain't about you! Engineering is a service-oriented business. "Silence is Golden." Ever hear that saying? Well sometimes in audio work settings it is better if no one notices you because it means that everything is going great. If you want the spotlight, find another occupation!

Do not stray far from work mode. Getting too comfortable in studio/creative situations without a direct invitation can be hazardous to your health and your work life. I know several engineers who focused on mixing up the client's marijuana when they should have been mixing the client's music. Out of work and missing their front teeth, they now realized the error of their ways.

Do not be a robot but learn how to blend in and still maintain a clear head for leading the creative actions of the room. The engineer is the set-up guy for every creative person who steps in the door to contribute. Respect the situation and always understand the responsibilities that go with the pay grade.

Whenever possible, get credit for your work. I always look at the credit as being just as important as the money in some cases. When I started, there were not many guys like me working consistently. I felt that doing gigs that brought little money but gave credit on a major project would help me later on. Today that view is a value judgment that each person must make. Many younger engineers feel that older established acts don't matter, so they don't take the credit seriously. Also, remember that when many of us started back in the day there was a definitive line that existed between producer and engineer. In today's environment, the line is gone and many are in competition for the same dollars. Therefore, credit and respect for who you are working with often takes a back seat.

And, for all those engineers who do not share because they feel that to share only risks them giving away precious information, think about this: Two people are engineers— one weighs 350 pounds and the other weighs 185 pounds. While a shared secret of audio may provide a hint in the right direction, these two individuals will never hear the same way! Unless someone possesses mutant powers such as those displayed by the X-Men, everyone's DNA is different. That would include their hearing signatures!

KNOW YOUR RIGHTS IN PROFESSIONAL SETTINGS

In 1999, I toured with a new artist who burst onto the scene with several hits on his first album. He had much expectation as he forged ahead on his second disc. The music director and I had worked with him since his first studio project. When tour time came we began to observe the many faces of his personality as the touring cast began to assemble. We got through rehearsals and were slated to begin a four-month-long tour that started in London and concluded in the United States. Everything went well in rehearsal, so we took off to London several days before the first show.

The days off in London were cool—we had great Indian food and saw the sights. To everyone's surprise, one day before our opening show we were called over to the artist's hotel for a meeting. We all gathered in a small meeting room that the hotel had provided. The tables were set up in the round so that everyone was in view of everyone else. As the band and crew awaited the artist and his manager, I thought to myself, be prepared for change because in entertainment nothing lasts forever, especially if you are in London with two days off!

Soon the artist and his manager came into the room. They sat down and the artist began with: "I am sorry . . . (tears) I can't do the tour . . . I need to get myself together!" That was followed with more tears and then he ran from the room.

After the artist's quick departure, the manager took over and said he would answer any questions. Shocked, many people's first response was to just look surprised and look to the manager as if he were going to say something more soothing.

I remember raising my hand and saying, "All of us want to see (the artist) get well and we feel for the weight of the position he is in. Now having said that, as his representative how are you prepared to deal with the question of lost revenue?"

While he may not have had the answer for me right there, what I needed was a verbal confirmation in front of everyone—band and crew. Canceling in Los Angeles would have been easy. Canceling in London seemed more like a strategy to me. At that point the shock on everyone's face was changed to individual concern about each of their households.

As this was going down all I could do was smile. The front of house engineer asked me why I was smiling. Here is why:

1. At that point it was about handling the business.

2. That question in a room full of people can only get an affirmative response or a riot.

3. Everyone's reaction instantly taught me how much the band and crew was *not* handling the business side of the business. In poker they call that a "tell."

4. I had my Tour Book.

Now here is an important fact for all you hopeful tour folks. A tour book is in fact a document, and/or paper trail, that provides proof of the existence of an employment agreement. Now do you realize why sometimes tour books are handed out late or sometimes not at all?

In the end we were reimbursed for a percentage of the lost time out on the road. The funny thing was that in no less than one hour after the emotional scene from the artist, he went right out in the fashion district to buy $50,000 worth of clothes and accessories. I guess he did get himself together!

Many people in a situation like that might choose to stay silent because of the fear of not being called back. If I had not spoken up in that room full of people, it would have given management a chance to individually tell each person whatever version of financial reimbursement truth that they wanted.

I knew that my way of looking at all potential work situations had paid off. I never go on tour unless I can cover the cost of getting home on my own. This makes it possible to not be held hostage by someone holding my plane ticket or playing with my money.

There is a whole separate strategy used in touring to acquire the support staff. Many approach it from a team perspective. Many have key people that they call to ensure the outcome. If you want to find out more about the tour world there are Websites dedicated to it. Talk to friends who tour. Understand that *the deal you cut is the deal you cut*. Also realize that with the large number of schools now specializing in the performance support aspect of the business, this area will soon be the new zone for corporate organizers to pre-qualify and market backline crews.

When you are on tour, you are working away from home for an artist at a rate that should make up for the fact that you are missing the opportunity to work at home. So you have agreed to be on tour and you have negotiated or agreed to a fee that gets you paid for doing shows.

Sometimes management will attempt to secure your services with a weekly reimbursement conversation. Then, when you get on the road, the conversation quickly turns to per show. A simple fax or e-mail can serve as proof as well. Always remember if it is business, commit it to paper.

I would also encourage you to investigate the rules regarding per diem. You can visit the state department's Website to get current per diem rates. This is another gray area that confuses many people. Know that it is a mandatory daily rate. I have seen many situations where management will say that you are out and only get paid per diem on show days. Being as informed as possible is the only way to get exactly what is yours when it comes to reimbursement for services.

Believe me, not everyone is out to get you but please be prepared for all kinds of verbal and linguistic re-direction in an attempt to sway you from your goal. How much do you want per seven-day week to be on tour? Ever since 9/11, the idea of going out and potentially losing your life for a two-hour show is a risk many do not want to deal with.

Touring is a great way to see the world and understand the power of the Arts. It is a good living and can open many doors for opportunity. I think there is no other pressure like the touring crew pressure. Each audience member is on the edge of his or her seat every night because an army of unknown support specialists called the backline crew have done their jobs to perfection. If you want the best results from this industry you need to bring your best every time you show up.

4

Follow Your Instinct

IF YOU FEEL SOMETHING IS WRONG, IT PROBABLY IS

Have you ever been in a car accident? Excuse the extreme analogy, but it helps make a point. Usually after the nervousness and sweating is done, you replay the thoughts you had surrounding the incident. You finally arrive at, "I should have followed my first thought and gone a whole different way."

That first thought that enters your mind, my friends, is called "instinct." Go left instead of right. Take your time and call to let them know you will be late instead of driving fast and unsafe. It is also the first thought that comes to mind when you meet someone and shake hands. I have been in business situations and thought, "I should not be here," and I should have followed my first instinct.

Anyone who has heard the term "working on spec" knows that this is a nice way of saying work at your own risk— the risk being that you might not get paid. A lot of this went on early in the business, and still does from time to time. Many times "creative deals" are based primarily in the land called "Spec." I know that back in the day we all did it as a way to get experience. Following your instinct helps you to make spec situations come about. Experience and knowledge move you on to the next project. I guess you could say that instincts help give birth to opportunity.

As I look back, sometimes I regret "instinctively" taking little money just to get in the door, even though in the long run it worked out. I think I regret it because nobody should ever have to dumb-down to get experience. As a black man with technical ability, race and the issues involved with it are a constant extra set of luggage that I, and every person of color, deal with in every area of life.

I always loved the questions I would get (mostly from white engineers) when I showed up to participate on a project: "Who are you and what have you done?" this day, I'm glad I followed my instinct in this next story:

I went for a dinner meeting with an artist and his wife, which came about because, as it turned out, we both had the same insurance agent, and the agent had referred me to them. When I got to the table, one of the engineers from his camp was there. We were introduced, and I extended my hand to shake. Then he immediately started with the normal line of questioning: "I've never heard of you, so what have you done? What qualifications do you have?"

I started to tell him my educational qualifications and then of the instruments that I helped to test while working in manufacturing. Then I listed clients. He quickly moved away from all the questions. The dinner meeting continued, and then I left. I remember that I was so involved in the dinner meeting at the time that the engineer's attitude did not even faze me.

No sooner did I get in my car than my cell phone rang and I was speaking with the artist and his wife. They apologized for their engineer's behavior and they understood if I didn't want to work with them. They said they had asked him to call me as well and apologize (which he did). Even though to me his approach seemed typical, I did not know that it was offensive to the people who employed him too. I was just following my instinct, which was to answer each question asked and meet some prospective clients over dinner—nothing more, nothing less.

I cannot say that this would have been my response when I started twenty years ago. I was so racially sensitive after college that I probably would have stopped the dinner meeting, kicked his ass, finished dinner, and then picked up the check. Instead I let his condescending behavior work against him. He was so arrogant to think that I had no business being there because he never heard of me. Well, I had never heard of him either. For me, race, prejudice, and the usual negative behavior associated with it have been an automatic set up for success. I also love the fact that most people do not understand that. In fact, I shared that story without telling you the ethnicity of the participants because "stupid" has no color, it just is.

This business is filled with arrogant people from all races in orbit around entertainers and their projects. These people are as necessary as the cool people. Why? Because the outcome of any project depends on the balance of good versus evil. The good people on the project will have good instincts, good intentions, and consistency. The bad people have good/bad instincts and are consistent at being themselves—a secondary level of distraction for all of those who are focused. Still, even their bad input may force you to look at a project in a different way and create something good.

Which one are you? Good or bad? I will give you a hint. If you possess a skill and talent that allows you to work anywhere in the world and produce a desired result, then you are probably one of the good ones. Now, if your first instinct was to wonder what it is that you do . . . well, I did say it takes all kinds!

Following your instinct will not only keep you safe, but it will help you to be a better steward of your time. In my early days I was always trying to get every call and be everywhere all at once. It just was not possible. Cell phones were new and too expensive for everyone to own. I had to learn the concepts that I share with you now the long, hard way.

I use my instincts in everything I do. I rely on them because I am in a business where I work with creative people. Creative people are by nature driven by feeling. As an engineer, instincts also help you forget the science and rules about audio and get into the sound and feel of the music.

How to Read People

Probably one of the most important skills that anyone can develop is the ability to read people. As a recording engineer, it's part of your job to be able to understand the creative atmosphere before anyone else in the room. This means that your job starts before the first note is played. It is evident in any setting when you pay attention and pick up details. As an engineer, when you pay attention, you can read the room, your artist, and every potential occurrence that happens when creativity and improvisation enter the session. This level of successful non-verbal communication is achieved by developing a close walk with your clients. When I say "walk" I am referring to the creative walk that takes place when they want to record. It helps to know how your artist understands music. As an example, some artists do not understand formal music composition and structure. They wouldn't know the benefits of playing with different styles of music or different musicians. It helps if you know their weaknesses. Some artists literally have to transform into a different person in order to enter their "creative" space. It helps to know if they enter that zone through pharmaceuticals or through natural means.

Some artists will be able to work better with selected musicians. I remember working with several artists who actually have a list of preferred musicians for every instrument. Some even have the same type of list for engineers as well, depending on the type of project they are doing. Whatever the case, my point is that you have to be looking for information in order to see it. Reading non-musical personal cues is something that all of us do. It could be a simple tapping of the foot during a solo, or it could be the glances between two musicians. The main thing to remember is that the more time spent noticing the details, the more trust will be instilled. Trust is one of the keys to great musical moments. As a live-mix engineer, the combination of trust and knowledge of the show material is what makes many live engineers' work stand out.

My good friend Scottie Pakulski has engineered for some of the biggest names in music. His success is based on several key factors:

1. He knows the talent on stage.

2. He knows the material.

3. He understands each of the rooms that he is playing in.

4. He has the trust of the talent.

Scottie mixed Prince's Musicology tour in 2004. The stage configuration was such that the sound system was literally firing out from all sides, with the band directly underneath. I remember the planning stages. Having worked with Scottie before, I knew he would make it work. His work on that tour was outstanding. His mixes were consistent night after night. I use this example to make this point. Scottie knew his skill set as well as the environment everyone was in. He got the best results because he used all the information at hand to set up the audience for a great show. Scottie has passion and he knows how to set the stage for musical moments to come front and center.

If you are working with a new artist, take the time to sit and talk to them about their career and find out how they got started. If you are working with someone who is already established, take the time to research their career and their creative music history before you sit and talk.

The art of observation also works when you are in a supervisory role. Knowing how to make your support staff want to do their very best is done by observing and then setting them up with the tools for success. As an engineer who is in charge, your job is to lead by example. You are as strong as the staff around you, so always remember the power and potential that you have every time you open your mouth. Always choose your words wisely.

Environment plays a big role as well. If people are comfortable, they will do just about anything. I recently spent some time with Allen Sides. He is one of the top pros in audio engineering, studio design, and someone I consider an expert in the evolution of the control room. As he was demonstrating his new monitor system, he went into great detail as each piece of music was played. I could feel his passion for his craft. This guy truly likes what he does and he conveys it in every action. As we looked around the control room we noticed that it had a very open design. I loved the fact that he did not conform to the same old standards. He had his own theory about how a control room should be used and he put his personal stamp on each one of his studios. Passion is infectious! As an engineer the passion and disposition that you show to your clients can make the session an event. Within events you will find moments. Get it yet? Passion is one of the keys to great musical moments.

While we are discussing the finer points of reading people, I would suggest everyone go buy the book *Making Records* by legendary producer Phil Ramone. It's filled with stories and valuable life lessons from one of our greatest living legends. Many of his descriptions of famous sessions and career memories contain great examples of how he reads both situations and people.

Taking the time to learn to read people can mean the difference between getting results and authoring confusion.

CALLING YOUR OWN SHOTS
. . . .

Don't Leave Now It's About to Get Good!

This story comes to me in reflection of my early years touring. Originally I tried touring to feel the pressure. Up until that point my career as an independent had been great and experience-filled, but I had never done anything live. Since I had clients who were musicians, I just waited for one of them to ask if I would be interested in going on the road.

It was great at first! Then, I began to see that a lot of guys on the road had never really experienced the other sides of the business. I also saw how the road changes people. It has been said, "Money amplifies who you are." Well I would say that money, opportunity, and mental instability all play equal roles! Not everyone is unstable but here is a story that shows how the ability to call your own shots really is an important asset.

One of my clients was a well-known keyboard player. He was going back out on the road with a legendary female singer. He asked if I was interested in going as his keyboard technician. I said yes and proceeded to go and meet with several of the management personnel. It was a very tight ship. Quasi family run you might say.

Anyway, we negotiated a rate and I joined the crew for several weeks of pre-production rehearsal. Pre-production is where the crew and band begin to assemble and work out all the elements of a show. The crew was young and many were from New York. At twenty-six I was one of the oldest and had a little more experience. This was not my first time on the road but unlike all the other backline staff I did not solely do tour work to make my living. I had several other private clients with facilities and I still used my electronics chops to do research and development work for new products and instruments being developed.

As we started to do our work, I began to notice that several of the guys in the crew were being replaced. I think I saw five Bass Techs lose their gig. I kept trying to get to know the guys but they kept changing so fast! Number five stayed the longest, and so far he seemed to be a nice guy. He and I were about the same age, and we both had families.

He knew that the bass player was hard to please. I watched this guy do things over and over and be criticized and berated, but he kept coming back to try again. We started the tour and began to build show experience together. Finally, one day on lunch he was standing outside smoking a cigarette and we were all talking about the tour dates. The bass player/music director pulled up. He gave his tech the nastiest look I had ever seen. The tech was fired that night after rehearsal. Why? Because he smoked on his break. He said he smelled like smoke. This same tech who had learned the show and was making a wage for his family was gone; not because he didn't do his job, but because he smoked. Whatever the case, I thought it was at the very least an unusual display of authority. He smoked when he first came to rehearsal. I guess his smell was delayed several weeks.

I went back to the hotel and thought to myself, if I am going to be with these people for some time I really have to want to be here. And from what I had observed I did not see the kind of allegiance that builds strong relationships. I had seen a Napoleonic leading style along with other qualities that I did not care to endorse by spending over a year of my life with them. I called the musician that had asked me to come out and I informed him of my intention to leave. He said, "That's funny because I'm leaving too because my album has just been released!"

I went in the next day and informed the management that I was leaving. I told them that I needed to do what I thought was best for my family and that while it might not make sense to them, I only ask that they respect my wishes.

Upon hearing the news, one of the younger members of the crew said to me, "Man you're leaving right when it's getting good! We are about to get free tennis shoes and sweat suits!"

I knew at that instant that I had made the right decision. As I was packing my work case, I pulled him aside to let him know that if I needed tennis shoes I could buy them. And that unlike him, I had a wife and two kids; I do this for real—not for extra spending money and free stuff. Being able to walk away or stay is powerful when it's your choice!

DO WHAT YOU DO

Avoiding Those Who Work at Nothing

This section was inspired by some words I read in Charles Barkley's book, *Who's Afraid Of A Large Black Man?* In particular, it was inspired by a quote from actor Samuel L. Jackson. He was speaking of the wide variety of jobs in the movie business and sharing other thoughts and views on the industry. The words I read were so true and resonated within me because I had felt this way as well. He said, "There is something right about people who work and there's something wrong about people who don't." He went on to say that "success breeds success."

The entertainment business is filled with folks who have perfected the art of doing nothing. It is visible at all levels.

When I started working in the studio, musicians actually got together and played without the aid of lawyers, managers, handlers, a posse, etc. While the need for legal advice and services has not really changed, I always noticed this trend—the more money someone makes, the more people they have around them to create situations that require their services.

Situational manipulation takes too much time and energy. You will find the lazy schemers are usually the ones who sit back and wait for the committed skilled laborer to actually do the work. By doing what you do, you will inevitably be faced with the true merit of the people around you.

For some time now, I have wondered why everyone is cool with this behavior. What I have come to realize is that it comes down to choice. People choose and allow all kinds of behavior around them as long as the results benefit them. It's called "go along to get along," and when it works, it's called good business and "the end justifies the means." When working in this industry as a service provider, you need to go to a real selfless place—a place where the only thing that you focus on is the completion of a task or project. Do not let personal desires get in the way. Never take for granted any area of influence that you might have. I like to give my clients the ability to choose at all times. Since I have read Jackson's words, I now look at everyone I meet in the business and think, "There is something right about people who work and something wrong about people who do not."

I have seen the concept of "doing what you do" come back to me. Once I was doing some work as a film score technician for a client, who at times was very snide and pompous towards everyone. I always let him be who he was and just solved his technical problems. At this time, when orchestras played big sessions they usually had two to three big synthesizer rigs on the scoring stage. One day his cartage guys set up his system wrong and a cable was loose. With the rig being so big he could not figure out what was wrong. He did, however, feel the need to panic and make a scene as his broken rig held up an entire orchestra date.

We were in front of some high-profile musicians and a very famous conductor/composer. As usual, there was no one like me there—I was "unique" (another term for being of color). This guy began to be loud and rude to me—the tech who was there to help him. I looked at him, listened, and then proceeded to fix the problem in under two minutes. When I finished, I said I would stay close until the end of the session. He was happy and went back to play.

After the session I waited until we were alone and said, "I am here to help you. I will not be spoken down to when I am the person you are relying on for technical support. I do understand your pressure; however, it does not look good when you conduct yourself like that. If it happens again, I'll walk out and not fix anything."

The next day I got a long apologetic phone call from him as well as a stronger relationship. The same day, I also got a call from another musician who was there and saw me take the bad attitude from the guy and then fix his rig. He said to me, "Dave everybody knows he's a prick. Don't worry! I was so impressed by the way you handled him. We all wanted you to pop him! I just wanted to know if you would come by my studio and do some work for me."

I cannot tell you how many times I have had my head down "doing what I do," and found out that someone was watching from a distance and saw the potential to do business with me.

My lifelong friend, Brian McCullough, is an engineer as well. He took my place when I left Herbie Hancock to work with Prince. He and I both try to reach back and look for the next guy who was like we were in college. I recently had Brian do a production manager gig for a local charity. He came in and did what we do. He lined up the sound system, met with the music director and event staff and prepped for the event. As usual, he encouraged some of the students attending our school's audio program to come and view the process up close by helping set-up. Upon viewing the work attitude of the students, the head of the rental company contacted Brian to get the phone number of one of the guys. He was offered and accepted his first professional job the next week. This guy just came to help set up and see the pro gear up close. No wage, no deal, just passion. His reward for coming was that opportunity met preparation. This student's manner stood apart from the others and the guy from the PA company asked specifically for him.

Sometimes what you do when you think no one is watching will speak volumes about who you are.

5

Reputations

Recently I finished a job that lasted about a year and a half. It was so intense that I actually relocated and set up shop in two different cities and commuted back and forth to Los Angeles. Upon the first weeks of arriving, a local musician and all-around good person befriended me. He was as familiar with my work as I was with his. It is a real blessing when you can actually meet some of the other folks in this industry who are not jaded by success or by the "illusion of inclusion" (that is being in orbit around someone who is popular by world standards). He is one of those guys who, if he called me and said, "I'm going to the moon on Tuesday," my response would be, "What do you need me to do?"

Anyway, for this job I was restoring an abandoned facility and I had asked him to help me find some local dealers that we could work with to get equipment. I did not want to upset the local business community that I might need later on by taking revenue out of state. Networking with dealers is a great thing. They make helping clients in remote locations a lot easier.

My friend introduced me to the owner of a local professional audio dealer. He had been familiar with the facility I was about to restore. I met with him and we discussed some of our needs as well as the history of what I will call "dealer abuse" (when dealers are left holding only invoices—no money and no equipment).

While I could not do anything about the negative invoice history, I extended my hand to say that I would personally guarantee that the things that I requested while I was there working at the facility would be paid for. I also told him he should contact some of the manufacturers that we both had dealt with to see whether or not I am a person who should be taken seriously. He did, and we began a great relationship. He was instrumental in getting me most of the gear I needed.

I tell you this story not only to show the power of my handshake and my word, but also to show the sequence of events. My word would have been nothing without the first introduction from our mutual friend. His word was good, and that allowed the dealer to look at me in a favorable light.

Here is another example of someone's word being enough. When I was in college I took advantage of a virtually unknown section of the school's catalog called "special major." This section was for people who knew what they wanted to do when they got out of school, but no formal block of classes existed for them. Part of doing a special major required the signatures of three professors. I had two and I needed one more.

One day I got an opportunity to second engineer for a well-known producer. During a break in the session he asked how I was doing in school. I told him I was doing well and that I was attempting to declare my "special major," but, I lacked the third letter of recommendation. He immediately picked up the phone and called a friend of his who was the audio department head of another local college. The next day I was handed a letter without even meeting the man.

The mysterious professor and I finally met in an elevator at a tradeshow about four years after the letter. At that point I had been working at Oberheim for a couple of years. I asked him why he wrote it without meeting me, and he said, "When I got the call, I knew if my friend said you were cool, then you were cool." Over the years we have worked together on many projects, and to this day, we are all still friends.

Sometimes a simple concept (such as your word meaning everything) can seem insignificant. In my early years I never really understood what my dad meant when he said, "Whatever you do, guard your name." I have come to learn exactly what he meant. It has been a struggle, but the more you learn, the longer you will survive in this business.

I used to worry a lot about my name and reputation. However, as I matured I came to accept that since I am truly about something and have been placed on earth in this industry at this time, then no negative behavior, scheme, or person can move me from what is mine.

Not everyone will like me and that is great. However, I have chosen to plant my seed in deep soil (relationships). I try to leave people smarter than when we met, and I like to give opportunities to all who show promise. I believe in win/win situations and the concept of a fair profit.

Word travels fast when bad business is in place. I know many vendors who, when they hear a name, will hoist red flags and sound a retreat. I remember going into that same dealer I mentioned earlier and asking for a rundown of local business folks who had represented themselves to be honest and fair. He quickly ran down the list and then gave me an idea of those who had a good amount of burned bridges behind them. People with bad reputations think they can screw people who they feel do not matter, but the so-called "little people" who make up this business are the ones who matter the most. Bad reputations travel faster than the speed of light, and it is harder to do business when you are known to have one.

We are at a time in history where even well-educated people have no real guarantee of "making it." The entrepreneur who understands the concepts of service, skilled labor, consistency, communication, and the strength of his/her word with a strong handshake to accompany it is well equipped to work in any environment.

ALLIANCES

Be Careful Who You Stand Next To

In addition to your name, your location and proximity to the action are also viewed from many angles. Those who use your services tend to view you in a crucially responsible role. They sometimes want you to function with as much ease and autonomy as they do. Always remember, being in a responsible role is what most people do not want. Most want to breathe the air next to the famous, but do not want to actually take on the workload.

I have always chosen to come aboard any situation and operate under a defined set of criteria. I will make the necessary crucial decisions that I have been asked to make and I will always do what I can to ensure that my client's issues become non-issues without fail, taking total responsibility for my actions in exchange for none of the financial responsibility. Translated simply, I can do my gig without the normal tools of power—control of the money.

That last point is what has steered many ships aground. I have worked in many situations where the person with the money was automatically given the power position. Everyone formed a nice neat "ass-kissing" line right around the corner and they proceeded to follow the fearless leader with the money and perceived power off the proverbial cliff.

Standing next to someone works both ways. I have worked with some clients for over ten years. When we go to tradeshows and other industry functions, people are accustomed to seeing us together. If they see someone recognizable and see me next to him or her, then we are linked together. That, in most cases, is the positive result of standing next to someone. Years of working together can add credibility to the relationship.

Here is the negative way that standing next to someone can impact you. Early on in my career, I was eager to work and took every call I got. I had one guy who would call and ask me the weirdest, most complex questions. I would always spend time giving him well-detailed answers. I was working so much that I could hear descriptions of problems and have a diagnosis that was right on point. In some cases, I knew the equipment so well that I could see the front panel in my head along with all the test gear on my bench. Anyway, this guy called me at least eight times in three months, and I got him his information each time.

About three weeks after his last call I was at a tradeshow and that same guy came up to me and started talking. Another gentleman walked up and started thanking him and praising his technical knowledge for two of the situations that I had advised him on. As it turns out, what happened was that the guy would leave the room, call me as soon as the problems became technical, and get the answer from me. Then he would go back in and act like he had worked it out!

I felt used and stupid—and that everyone knew how I was taken advantage of. I did not get mad and make a scene. I took everything in and the next time he called I just said, "I don't know." Or, if he hailed me in a public setting, I stayed away. I realized that in a public setting he wanted to be perceived as working with me. My inner strength came from knowing that my knowledge came from years of real work, not phone tricks and visual attempts at validation.

I do understand that, depending on the situation, I can lend my own personal credibility to anything going on.

After so much time in the business and working in all environments, it is necessary for you to understand how those around you perceive you and your work. I still go to tradeshows with clients, although in the long run I prefer to stand with my wife and kids—it is safer that way.

6

Commitment Versus Involvement

I heard an interesting analogy once that stuck with me all these years. It has to do with the difference between the pig and the chicken. You see in order to get a nice plate of bacon and eggs, both animals had to provide the raw materials. Here is where the difference lies:

* The chicken was **involved**, laying the egg and moving on to lay more eggs another day.

* The pig was **committed,** giving his life for each slice of bacon provided.

Much like the pig and chicken, we as independent engineers are faced with the same choice when it comes to our clients and our way of creating work and interacting with the marketplace. If we choose to be involved, we are often times waiting for others to give signals before activating our skill set. If we commit then we do not have to wait for others to initiate an action. That committed attitude is sometimes referred to as being proactive. It shows itself in how close you pay attention to clients' needs and to the details of the project. Experience will be the only teacher that tests you every time you work.

This story is so recent that it is still hot. I just finished a consultation on a large commercial voiceover studio complex. We had been called after a well-known designer had been there and dictated to the owners what they must do to get the results they wanted. I received a call from the owners who said they had gotten my number from someone in the industry and that they wanted me to meet with them and give my professional opinion. My first meeting was just to view the new building and meet with the owners.

The site was a two-story office building on one of the busiest streets in Los Angeles. After viewing the property and taking photos, I sat down with the owners and asked them what they would like me to do. I wrote down everything they were asking for and asked them about the budgets associated with each area. We also discussed the timeline, as they still were doing business while moving locations.

They had already secured a contractor and an architect, so they needed me to work with the architect and come up with a plan for the studio that could be built within the specified time. We created a calendar and crafted a solution that worked. I provided all the specialty information for the studio's acoustic needs and the architect provided all the drawings that allowed for city permits to be pulled and construction to begin.

After the first meeting I began to research and build a file on the job. We arranged to meet later in the week and discuss the gear with one the studio's outside technical support people. I arrived early for the meeting and discussed setting up a schedule and how to best make studio decisions with their chief engineer.

As he and I exchanged information, the studio tech arrived late, sat down and proceeded to ask me a litany of questions regarding the studio's designs which had not yet been decided. I listened and waited to get back to the real purpose of our meeting—the equipment and technical needs of the design. We never got to it. Instead, he continued to take us all on a trip through his unique approach to his support role as the studio tech. I finished the meeting and let the owner know that I thought they should have everyone involved in agreement about what they would like to do, and then I would feel better about proceeding. I told them that I did not want to waste time on meetings like that again.

As I went to my car, the chief engineer came out and apologized for the tech's behavior. I told him that there was no need to do that because we had bigger issues to solve together (completion of the new facility). I found out later that the tech was the same guy who referred the former studio designer to the owners. He had told them they could not have successful functional studios on the second floor.

Here is where the committed and the involved portion of the story are most evident. If both the tech, who had an existing business relationship with the studio, and the designer were committed to the client, I would have never gotten the call on a referral in the first place. Due to the fact that I do not use business cards and all my business is by referral, whenever I get a call, I am committed to the call, the first meeting and anything else that has made its way to me. I am committed to envisioning the big picture to see if we can work together.

Instead, those two chose to waste time trying to raise the price of the job and talk the owners into something they were not willing to do. Many support service people make this mistake. It is no different than bidding a job based on address rather than true cost. Business settings and attitudes about service and sincerity have changed drastically since the fall of Enron. For years everyone thought that the guys in the suits knew better. The guy in the suit may only know where to buy nice clothes. The guy or gal who can give you good service looks like the rest of us.

The tech made a second mistake by wasting time testing me in front of the owners. He should have been cooperative and used time wisely. I had no problem answering questions but he missed the point of the meeting. The owners had already decided and laid out what they wanted, so we came to the meeting on time looking forward to making progress. Instead, he brought the meeting to a halt with a panic management strategy, trying to prove that he knew a lot.

Because he was only **involved** with his clients and not committed to the business at hand, he damaged whatever relationship he had built while operating as a tech for them.

The studio designer who was referred at first had made it real clear that whatever the outcome, a first meeting with him would cost five-hundred dollars. His major mistake was that he had no long-term vision and he did not listen to what the owners wanted. If he had listened he would have heard that they had been in business successfully for over twenty years in a studio they originally built by themselves.

That one point deserves respect at the very least. Here is why. While he is an expert in studio design, he was not an expert at closing the deal. He spent his concentrated energy telling the potential new client that he needed five-hundred dollars just to talk. Then, upon arrival he told the potential client that unless they did exactly what he said to do that nothing else would be possible.

Did he forget that even though these guys were not studio designers, they had built their own space twenty-plus years ago and prospered without him, his expert opinion, or his five-hundred-dollar meeting fee? Both the tech in this story and the studio designer probably know a lot and have done some great work . . . somewhere.

Here is the other thing. That job was never theirs because they did not really want it bad enough. One thing I learned from working with many high-profile clients is that you never waste everyone's time by discussing what is not possible. Never have long discussions about what is **not** going to happen. People who have the finances in place to hire professionals from different areas did not get in that position by focusing on the negative aspects of their work. When you waste a client's time, they will notice.

As the job progressed, I met with the architects, structural engineers, air-conditioning specialists, electricians, construction contractor, and carpenter and we all developed a plan that worked out quite well. It worked well because we all had **committed** to finish.

Many times ego gets in the way of making good decisions. I have found that many support contractors in our business seem to have this attitude. Back in the day when technology was new and there were fewer people to compete for service situations it was possible to use the "charge what the market will bear" strategy. Today, we have an educated consumer. I have found for example that many wiring technicians like to come in and talk over the client's head, as if they are designing the next "Mars Probe" when the modern-day studio is sometimes (not always) literally a point A to point B conversation. This type of arrogance leads many to lose out on jobs that they never had in the first place. No potential client ever wants force-fed service.

Here is a hint: If you want to get more from your opportunities then take the time to look up and learn about the people who you are providing service to. Listen instead of talking.

The one thing that proves itself to me over and over again in this business is that truly committed people will never be stopped. None of us had ever worked together before, but the result of our collective effort was and still is unstoppable.

When the time came we all did the work required and in the end the client was very satisfied. To see the facility, go to www.radio-ranch.com.

7

Picking Clients

ALL CLIENTS ARE NOT THE SAME

All aspects of our business have one thing in common—they are all about serving the client. Of course, some clients are easier to deal with than others.

I have always made a point not to advertise or use business cards. Over the years my work has all come from recommendations and referrals. Of course, it was not always that way. In the beginning, my only hope was that my phone rang every day. Fortunately, it did. In the process of doing jobs and turning new clients I would get referrals as one client gave my number to another. This is an old-fashioned method, but it does help to identify those who are serious about working with you. Remember, I started at a time when the Internet was still in development, so potential clients could not Google "audio engineer" or "sound technician" to find my home page.

The nice thing about referrals is that the leads tend to be more reliable. Of course, that does not necessarily mean the client is going to go easy on me. Here are two stories I wish to share that best exemplify that all clients are not the same.

I remember having a new client who was a referral. He was a film guy who was very nice before we started working together; however, his attitude changed as soon as we started the project. It seemed to me that he was trying to find fault and was unnecessarily confrontational. I kept having conversations with him over small details. He kept making changes and expecting me to eat the cost. It seemed as though he was trying to make me look bad in front of the guy who referred me.

When I talked with the guy who referred me, he said something to me that let me see the error of my ways. He explained, "Everyone is different, and this guy has no appreciation for people beyond their professional use." I was giving him the same treatment that I did the guy who referred me, who had been a good client for years. For me to extend this new client favors—which would cause me to lose money on the project—was, in essence, a self-inflicted wound. One that once I realized what I was doing, could easily be fixed.

Just as service providers have to gain the trust and respect of clients over time, we should make clients do the same. Never give a client the same props as the guy who referred him. At a certain point, "All must earn their stripes" as they say. Be very cautious of clients who change their tone once money changes hands. Some people cannot be pleased. Sometimes they do not make sense, and are so caught up in their own perceived power that they lose sight of reality. When you are in the service business you work **with** people and not **for** them. There is a difference.

I remember another time when a musician called me to do some work. This was someone I admired, and was actually excited about the prospect of meeting him. I told a couple of my other well-known clients, and they all made the same comment: "Make sure you get all your money." My first thought was, "Hmm, interesting comment," but I thought nothing of it.

We started to work together, and three fourths of the way through I got a letter stating that I had "held up his project for some time, and he was not paying my back-end." The truth was that I was ahead of schedule by two days and that was just a form letter that he always used to get out of paying back-end fees. I discovered that it was a form letter because I ran into someone who had gotten the same letter, and had gotten cheated out of his back-end as well.

Luckily for me the one thing that I had done correctly was to get a 70 percent deposit for the job to start.

This is now my standard practice for all who need service but seem to carry the essence of "bad vibe." Seventy percent up front is also a figure that some will think twice about before acting a fool or trying to steal services for free. As we know, with excessive budget sometimes comes excessive behavior. With that in mind, never feel bad about creating terms that make you happy about proceeding in a situation.

Remember, if you are going to be a service provider in the entertainment business, at a certain point you are your own company, whether you are incorporated or a DBA (more on that in Chapter 12). You will not get through your career without your share of nightmare client stories. I have been blessed to have very few of those stories, yet I have reviewed every one of them so I could see what I needed to change about myself to make sure that they did not happen again.

No matter how unreasonable the other person was, you have to take some responsibility for the situation. When things go wrong you have to ask yourself, "What role did I play in this?" Then use the experience to steer clear from those kinds of situations as well as modify your own behavior.

SELECTING JOBS

Some Kind of Money Costs Too Much to Make

At one time or another I think that all of us have been somewhere or did something in work or in life that we know we should not have done. I heard the term "selective amnesia" from a friend of mine when we were reflecting on some past clients. We both had recently done our share of work helping an artist transition his recording environment from his large off-site studio to a home studio. Looking back at the job, we found a pattern that seemed to show up in many of our clients. They seem to only really need you when they need you. As you begin to solve their needs, they get that "selective amnesia," and only remember the things they want to.

There were a couple of years when producers from other countries with accents were in style. All of a sudden we had a run of guys from across the water talking funny and making some hip music. I would always be amazed at how these guys approached me. They would usually call and say, "I hear that you did (some other client's name) work at his studio. Well, I need to do the same thing; however, I want to add this and this."

The interesting thing was that they could say what they wanted clearly, and seemed to understand everything perfectly until it was time to pay, which they were slow to do. On top of that they often figured their service calls were free. Suddenly there was a language barrier.

Their accent, while different, only added spice to the same BS that their American counterparts served up. Most of the time they wanted to understand how others in this country worked and completed projects. They would have done better to ask me questions and pay me for talking, rather than hiring my services! It would have been a less expensive education for them.

My friend and I reached the conclusion that our bad times were just as much our fault as it was the clients'. We decided at that moment to always examine the jobs that came our way. Now when we get a call, no matter who it is, we both have a process we use to accept or turn down the gig. Many times I have turned down gigs from well-known entertainers. When asked by associates, "Why didn't you do that gig man?" My response was always the same: "Some kind of money costs too much to make." Too much wasted time and too much non-musical activity. It costs too much when the drama outweighs the experience.

Most clients thank me for being cool under pressure or handling things. What they do not realize is that I have paid a large price for my patience and tolerance of artistic behavior. My blood pressure is high as hell and most of the time I want to go postal on all those who are inconsiderate around me. I have worked in many camps and have seen the collection of angels and devils that work side by side to make this business what it is. At forty-six, I am just now getting to claim my whole day for myself and the things that I find important. Hopefully, by reading this, you can figure it out sooner in your own career.

I find that our business is filled with greedy, negative, lazy, powerful, friends of friends. Everyone wants to show off and no one wants to work. The next generation of dealmakers is not really concerned with passing info on; they merely want to win at any cost. They have no style—just a "gangster-like" attitude toward the industry. Assistants and managers act as tyrants and keep the artists secluded like their own personal piece of veal—tied up and in the dark!

This next story is a testament to that. Recently my wife and I took on some editing work. We were at home one evening when we got a call from another engineer that I have known for over twenty years. He told us he was on a project and what they needed was more engineers to finish editing an audio book.

We went down to meet with the producer and see if we would be the right fit for what they needed. We listened to what they had to say and discussed the rate for our time and the rental of our equipment. The project had historical implications and could possibly be a great source of African American historical information for years to come.

While we were excited to get to work on the project, several key things were missing—the first being a plan. One thing that was evident to us was that the producer had limited, if any experience with the type of production that she was undertaking. Each time we asked a question about the direction, we got a vague answer and a quick redirection to issues not in discussion. Sometimes the hardest thing for many to say is, "I don't know."

Time and deadlines were working against them. All the engineers on the project decided to take chapters and complete them. They also started adding sound effects and music. The engineer who called us had been on the project the longest and he was brought on to assemble everything and mix the final product, however he had gotten stuck editing because nothing was ready to mix. We agreed to a start time for the next day and went home.

The next day when we were setting up our gear I asked my friend the lead engineer, "This seems like a simple project. Why is it taking so long?" That is when he told me that the producer was literally chasing people away from the project with her lack of knowledge and condescending behavior. She would come in and stand over people and ask, "Why are you doing that? How come it's taking so long?"

I had seen this style of panic management production before. I was surprised with all of the big names that were attached to the project that it was being run this way.

Nevertheless, we worked hard to make progress. By the end of the first day several chapters had been done and we had started to add sound effects.

Eventually, the producer's style was focused on us and our contribution that day. She was persistent in asking us when we thought it would be finished. My answer without hesitation was, "How long did it take you the last time you did something like this?" She finally admitted that she had never done anything like the project before.

That is when I let her know the details of the production process from an engineering perspective. She had been recording vocals whenever she felt. She had recorded the same person in different studios, with different microphones, and no notes. So upon playback all her audio files sounded different. Not so good when you have famous people reading with recognizable voices. I explained that it takes twice as long to cut up and edit so that the final mixer is not stuck trying to match and hide all of the mistakes made earlier during the capture process.

I also explained that since she had not selected all of the elements to each chapter like music and sound effects, that we all would have to stop and double back to each chapter for placement. Under all those circumstances, we could only be done as soon as she had finished all her work.

The producer could have gotten finished quicker if she had hired everyone after she had her elements figured out and then laid out a real plan on completion. Instead, we were all on a trip inside her scattered head to figure out what she wanted to do.

In her ignorance of the process she also wasted time trying to pit all the engineers against each other by questioning their skills and speed. What she did not realize was that we all spoke to each other about what she had said about each of us behind closed doors. It backfired because she ended burning bridges everywhere she turned. After three days we decided the money was costing too much to make.

In the time we were on the project, we helped them regain significant lost ground. We met with the producer to let her know that they should be able to finish easier and that we would not be returning. Her way of treating us and the people around us ultimately led us to believe that we truly had better things to do with our time.

People like that producer cannot identify and do not appreciate what well-trained engineers bring to the project. They are more interested in ordering takeout food and playing producer rather than letting everyone do their best. When you are given the decision-making role of producer, it is never a question of *who* is in charge. The question is *how* in charge are you?

Always take the time to examine everything about every situation that you get exposed to. I have always believed that there is a secondary purpose that brings all of us together who work in this business. When the timing is right, the result of the collective work effort is unforgettable. I have been fortunate enough to work consistently for many years, and I have always found more lasting information during the trip than I did at the destination.

8

How Do I Really Get a Job?

Imagine someone asking you, "Hey, how do you make your money?" It has happened to me on many occasions. I think it is funny when people are so comfortable with you that they will ask you something like that. The other statements I love are "Man how do you get all the calls?" and "You are so lucky!" I paused and thought to myself. Why shouldn't I get the calls? Has my twenty-five plus years of doing audio of every kind been some massive con job? If my getting calls for jobs is luck, then what are all the skilled people doing?

The bottom line is this: I have work because on my way up I gave work and opportunities to others. There were times that I could not or would not do gigs. Instead of just saying no, I referred someone. I tried to match the client's disposition with that of a person I thought would make their situation very productive. Since I did not use business cards, I knew that if they came to me, they valued my participation and they got my phone number from someone who knew me and the services I provide. I passed the same opportunities on, just as it had been done for me. Even today, I will give work to those individuals who show themselves to be truly service oriented.

Today, many engineers complain about the lack of work. This is very similar to musicians who used to complain about lack of sessions. Back in the day, everyone was comfortable with the studio system when record companies were paying the bill. I saw many musicians realize too late that they had squandered time waiting for calls when they should have been writing original music and learning to read charts better. When you are an engineer, album work is not the only work available to you! These skills can be expanded and crossed over to many other potential work situations. Remember, "content" comes in many forms.

By the very nature of its behavior, our industry created many people who work consistently year after year on projects of all types. They develop their own clientele and manage to get on some special projects every now and then. These people make relationships count and have grown their client base from the ground up. They make their own non-traditional path to get in the door, and sometimes they even make the door. When they do get to contribute on a project of a known artist, the result is never a surprise to us because they had been doing the work and practicing the craft. Ask any engineer about the stuff they recorded that never saw the light of day. We have all done those sessions. It is only after your first ten years that you realize that some of the early projects were just for your educational or experiential benefit.

When you generate your own work and are not waiting for inclusion in group activity, you actually set yourself up for a greater chance for consistent business. The exclusive old boy network now looks at the industry that has no money to give them and says, "We need a new business model; there is no money available at this elite level we created!" Meanwhile back at the ranch, the rest of us regular folk are steady at work on the projects that we created with those clients we started relationships with when we first realized we were not being included.

So, who is better and does it really matter? Is the rich kid with all the gear the best or is the guy who has limited resources and works every day on whatever he can? Both are good. It is about who is right for the job. The kid with all the gear might be great at the technical aspect of being an engineer. In addition he has "access." While his abundance of gear may give him a tactical advantage, his personality is not for every situation.

As usual, the guy with limited means is the sleeping giant, he can usually work in more situations due to the fact that his career is guided by a "Rocky-like" work ethic. Those of us who came from limited resources (isn't that a nice way to say poor?) understand the freedom that exists in the absolute reality of having nothing. Let's apply this to our careers today and the state of our industry. There are more independent situations today than ever before. If you apply yourself you can actually find several situations that are just for you.

Try to do as much work as you can. Talk to people; give back to the industry by focusing on someone other than yourself. When you talk to people, listen to what they say. Within their responses you will usually find information as to what they or others might need. Take the time to understand the business as well as mentor others as you become more experienced.

When you get work please get it because you are sincere about doing a good job. Do not be like some people who berate the work of others to create an employment opportunity. I remember a production team from New York who used the same process whenever they went to an artist's private studio facility. They always had the same comment, "Our studio is much better." That form of closure for business is risky and very tricky. Those particular guys successfully redirected the workflow to their studio and associated billable services; however, in the end their efforts to produce a hit fizzled and their costs overran the budget.

Do not use your technical knowledge to create job security or extort time and money from clients. Creative people are taking the time to educate themselves these days so you would benefit more from being truthful. You would be surprised at how strong your creative relationship can grow. You might also be surprised at how much your clients will appreciate your working *with* them as opposed to your *telling* them what to do.

Look how technology has increased the productivity rate for content development. This will help you be a better steward of your time. Become more efficient and less opinionated. Many experienced engineers waste time offering their opinion on everything. I once worked with a great musician who told an opinionated live engineer, "So what? Who cares what you think?" When (insert artist name) is making a record, they are not thinking about you, so shut up!

As my good friend Dr. George Shaw says, "It's a business of friends." He tells all of his students this and has done so for over twenty years. I know it is a fact because he was one of the first people who opened the door for me and we have worked together on some very musically historic projects. When I lecture at audio schools, the biggest concern from students seems to be how they will pay bills and survive when they get out of school.

Many people who have chosen an audio engineering education will never have a class called, "How to Handle Life after Graduation." No school can promise an employment situation upon graduation, especially because it is up to you to get out there and make something of yourself. For this reason I offer you the following tips to getting a job. These can be applied whether you are independent, student, or educator.

- While in school impress your instructors as well as anyone you come across or work with. These people will be the first ones in your database.

- Read all kinds of material that will increase your vocabulary and make you well rounded when conversing with others. Practice writing, being able to communicate your thoughts clearly on the written page helps you to speak better as well.

- Constantly be around audio events, music, and special functions. You want to be at any activity where audio skills are required and where content is being created. You never know who you will meet.

- Take work that you might not consider glamorous, even jobs that you might not want to do forever. You never know what opportunities it can lead to. Every opportunity you take will allow you to meet more people. As an independent contractor, every person you meet is a potential client or reference.

- Start building your personal brand while you learn your craft. The world moves at such a fast pace right now that you have to include your brand development right alongside your daily workload. Your "brand" is your reputation in the professional community. It is your responsibility to uphold it and increase its awareness.

- Be a team player at all times.

- Never pre-judge anyone as unimportant; you never know who you are talking to in this business. Having an attitude of arrogance or entitlement will most certainly cut off your opportunity to work, build your brand, or be of service.

- Use the Internet to research, educate, and update yourself on a daily basis. Information can be used many ways. You could go to job websites and see how many jobs you are interested in, or you can go to those same sites and see what kind of jobs come up most often. The second method will tell you where the need is in the industry. If you want to create your own niche then begin to look at and process information several ways.

- The Websites that I will supply are a big help in the search. As an independent, remember not to be afraid to create your own method for finding work.

Remember the intention is to do what you love. In this case it's audio engineering so the immediate goal for the inexperienced is to get a job, and the long-term implication is to have a career.

- Never ever give up!

INTERNET RESOURCES

Listed here are some Websites as well as some other resources that will help you as you begin to use your skills as an audio engineer. At these sites you will find a salary calculator to use in figuring out what an audio engineer in your area can make. Go to www.about.salary.com or www.payscale.com. Follow the instructions and it will give you the relevant numbers to target in determining your worth and making a living in your area of the country. These are only guides.

Remember the following:

(A) You still have to do the work.

(B) What you make is up to you in the end.

(C) Many situations may potentially require a creative deal.

These sites can help you locate employment opportunities where your skills can be used:

Applause Music Careers: www.cnvi.com/applause

Entertainment Careers: www.entertainmentcareers.net

Entertainment Jobs: www.entertainmentjobs.com

Maslow Media Group: www.maslowmedia.com

MIDI and Audio jobs: www.midi.org

Showbiz Jobs: www.showbizjobs.com

TV Jobs: www.tvjobs.com

Vault: www.vault.com

These sites are for live sound and touring information. Use them not only to find work, but to begin developing your professional database.

IATSE: www.iatse-intl.org

LA411: www.la411.com

Gig List: www.giglist.org

Backstage Jobs: www.backstagejobs.com

Roadie Jobs: www.roadiejobs.com

Roadie: www.roadie.net

Roadie Show: www.roadieshow.com

Rigger's Page: www.rigging.net

Other resources for audio engineers include these sites:

NARAS: www.grammy.com (Producers & Engineers wing)

SPARS: www.spars.com

Mix Magazine: www.mixonline.com

Record Label Resource: www.recordlabelresource.com

Pro Sound News: www.prosoundnews.com

Electronic Musician: www.emusician.com

Audio Mastermind: www.audiomastermind.com (database)

eSession: www.esessions.com

Take the time to contact NARAS and your local chapter of the Recording Academy. The Producers and Engineers Wing of the Grammy's is there for your benefit. It's real important to get involved in the work of NARAS. If you are passionate about your ideas for the industry and you feel like you could make a difference, look into it. Many people do not even know the good work that is done at the Recording Academy.

Develop a Web presence for yourself as well. That is necessary for potential clients to access you from all points of the globe. As your experience increases, so will your need to work with others. You cannot expect to yield the results you wish unless you embrace current forms of communication and marketing. Somewhere there is someone trying to do something that you have some experience in. The Internet helps you reach new markets. With a Website you do not need to have long conversations. People can find out about you then contact you if they feel you are right for the job. No more passing out cards, no more trying to sell when what you do is service.

The following listings are examples of jobs just as they are posted. Look at the skills needed section of each. Then, decide honestly if you can perform the work required.

Recordist: This is a part time job
Location: Los Angeles, CA
Date Posted: 1/17/2008

Details: Prime time Emmy winning reality / documentary / variety sound facility is seeking a part time recordist. Primarily evenings and possible weekend and day shifts.

Responsibilities:
- ADR recording
- Foley recording
- Voice Over / Narration recording
- Client interaction and accommodation

Requirements:
- Minimum of 5 years experience in post production sound (television).
- Strong client relation skills.
- Mastery of Pro Tools.
- Strong computer skills PC & Mac.
- FTP, ISDN and Phone Patch proficiency.
- Excellent follow through, communication and organizational skills.

Salary: $30.00 per hour

Music Studio Engineering ADR, Song, Score:
This is a FULL TIME JOB
Location: Malibu, CA
Date Posted: 1/13/2008

Details: We are looking for an exceptional studio engineer who has ADR experience, jingles, score, and enjoys a busy schedule. You will track talent, record ADRs, record to time code for TV and Video production, and more. If the candidate has video experience it's a major plus. The schedule might be flexible, as in a four day week, depending on the work load.

Must have extensive engineering experience, or a young wiz. Fast, yet competent, knowledgeable in ProTools, DP, 5.01, and easy to work with.

Salary: Negotiable.

Re-Recording Mixer: This is a FULL TIME JOB
Location: North Hollywood, CA
Date Posted: 1/23/2008

Details: Seeking experienced re-recording Pro-Tools mixer for busy television production company. Various docu-soap/reality shows for a variety of networks.

Must be proficient in 5.1 Surround, Archiving, Audio Laybacks/Print stems, Dolby Surround, Mastering, Mixing, Pre-Dubbing, Sound Editing, Sound FX Editing, Synching.

Duties to include audio mixing and clean up. Printing stems, back ups, reconfiguring audio layouts for various deliverables.

Salary: To commensurate with experience.

THE DEAL YOU GET IS WHAT YOU ASK FOR

Let this poem be a reminder to you that you get what you ask for. Nothing more, nothing less.

The Deal

I bargained with life for a penny and life
would pay no more,

However I begged at evening when I counted
my scanty store.

For life is a just employer, He gives you what you ask,

But, once you have set the wages, why, you
must bear the task.

I worked for a menial's hire, only to
learn, dismayed,

That any wage I had asked of life, life would
have willingly paid.

Poem courtesy of Grammy Award-winning engineer Ralph P. Sutton

9

Knowing Your Value

HOW MUCH SHOULD YOU CHARGE FOR YOUR SKILLS?

This section contains some practical ways to look at and create your individual fee schedule.

When I was in trade school I remember hearing a teacher say, "After one semester in this program you will be worth no less than $12.50 per hour." What he was saying was that the technical knowledge a person attains is worth a certain amount of money on the open market. If we were to leave school after just one semester, we should not take less than $12.50 per hour.

As I progressed through college and my first work experiences, I began to see other things as well:

1. Most people who have a steady job are worth more than they get paid.

2. Most households are two to three paychecks from being broke.

3. Even if I got a corporate job, how could they keep paying me what I am worth forever?

Come to think of it, I really had entrepreneurial tendencies as far back as I can remember. Hell, I even played by myself when I was a child. It is a special calling to own your own business. I have been blessed with skills and a good nature as well as the technical knowledge that I learned in school.

One of the keys to knowing your value is to know the pay scales that are associated with all the areas in which you have expertise. Below is a partial description for four categories of work. Most of the work I do will fall into one of these four.

Technical work. . . . . Technical rate
Engineering work. . . . . Engineering rate
Studio design work. . . . . Studio design rate
Consultation work . . . . Consultation rate

Within each of these categories are several areas of
specialization. Over the years, as my number of jobs
increased, so did my second tier list of specializations.

Technical:	Keyboard Tech
	Computer Tech
	Stage Tech
	Studio Tech
	Custom Electronics
Engineering:	Studio Engineer
	Live Engineer
	Mix Engineer
Studio Design:	Contractor
	Electrical Design
	Systems Design
	Room Design
	Construction
	Acoustic Design
Consultation:	Tour
	Recording Studio
	Personal Creative Space
	Industrial Environments
	Special Projects

Whenever I have a meeting regarding the possibility
for me to work, I usually find that any situation will fall

into one of these categories. Everyone's table will look different depending on his or her education and work experience. My fee schedule is directly tied to the first four categories.

The method you use to determine your worth is simple once you outline who you are and put it in front of you. If I go to the first four original categories, they give me an idea for what pricing is by their description. Engineering and technical work are, by nature, specializations, and take some amount of schooling and experience to achieve reliability.

Studio design and consultation, by description, have a longer timetable involved. They also require a design/consultation fee. Remember the earlier discussion we had about spec work? You could, for example, start a record on spec—record a demo in hopes of getting a real budget (paid) later on. However, you could not design a studio or consult on spec. These projects involve commitment for heavy responsibility at the very start.

FIND YOUR RATE

Here is an exercise I created to illustrate a point: List the things you do very well on a sheet of paper. Now you can see what you have to offer. At this stage in your career, the page may be fairly blank.

I say that not to be mean but to be real. Most people do not jump into any field at the top. Be realistic in your assessment of what you have to offer. Be fair, but do not sell your talent short. A fair wage is a good target to aim for when negotiating. For those of you just leaving school with plenty of training but no track record, be ready to make creative deals to get your first gig.

When you have training but no experience, it is a good idea to take unpaid internship positions. When you start in that position, a potential employer can tell if you are worth the time and risk of adding you to the payroll. That would be your chance to present a reliable, hard work ethic. With time management, you could take different internships to find your niche.

Some of you might already know that you want to have your own recording facility. If that is the case, then I suggest, along with writing your business plan, you take a job at a successful recording facility. Then you can see what work, as well as what revenue, is available at that end of the business. Famous studios have great reputations for a reason. Remember that success breeds success.

If you want to do tour work and you were going out for the first time as an instrument tech, would you jump at an offer of $600/week? The answer is *no*. Investigate the live tour industry and find out what backline instrument techs make. Contact your local PA rental company. Find out what their responsibilities are. See if you could do it. Changing a broken guitar string in your garage is not the same as changing one in the dark in an arena full of fans at a crucial time in the show.

GETTING PAID

Just as you learned the basics of music, recording, software programs, hardware, etc., you need to learn the laws of business and the procedure on getting paid.

Getting paid brings us to another part skipped by most. Closure refers to ending up at a negotiation for services. If you are working for a company, human resources and the accounting department usually handle any money issues. If you work with an individual, sometimes these issues are handled by the principal themselves, then handed to others to carry out the paper functions. If you are an independent contractor, all your basic conversations should confirm the following activity:

- What do you need from me? What is expected of me?
- How much do you have to work with?
- When do you need it completed?
- Where do I have to perform my service?

Normally negotiations start at the first call. At that time you should say your basic rate for service. However, if it looks like the project might lead into some unforeseen costs or time, be careful not to price yourself into a corner. You need as much information as possible to really quote a price. It's okay to take some time to figure it out and get back to them with a price.

Sometimes the job is cut and dry and you might have a standard price. Make them aware of your price, but if you do not spend more than thirty minutes on the first visit, do not charge them. They will remember that you came, solved their problem, and cut them some slack. I always liked telling people to call me when they really had a problem, or sometimes I would say, "No charge, just give my name to ten people." Whatever you choose to do, please employ your own style and it will work fine. Have no shame in discussing money or asking for what you are worth.

Upon reaching a conclusion, *put it on paper*. Any true businessperson will not be afraid to put on paper what they are vocalizing. Commitment to paper is the first step toward agreeing that there is work to be done. You will find that the "put it on paper" principle will follow you throughout your life, way beyond business.

When you negotiate, the smallest amount of information in any one of these areas can help you figure out situational financial possibilities, even when the person on the other side is being evasive. Being evasive usually means that person doesn't have all the facts.

It is really important to know what you truly need. Do not attempt to enter the entertainment business with loads of outside issues that turn into excuses and special stories later on. Knowing how much it costs for you to live on earth every day is an important piece of information. It is the basis for maintaining a peaceful home environment. Figure out how much you need to bring in on a daily/weekly/monthly basis. This helps you map out how you will work in your chosen career and it will help you enjoy your life.

When you know about the project and are setting up your payment schedule, decide if it will be per project, per day, per hour, or a weekly rate. Be sure to include how many hours you will put in. You have to be aware of what the gig will be demanding from you and price it accordingly. Here is a general business procedure that should be somewhere in the conversation before work begins:

Agree—let the client know that you will write down everything you talked about and you both can look at it before you begin work.

Put it on paper—this can be in short letter form on your company letterhead stating your service intentions for the job.

Create a dated invoice that includes:

1. Your company (if you have a business, include your Employer Identification Number) and contact info

2. Their company and contact info

3. The terms or agreement for service

4. The payment or compensation

5. Payment schedule (whether it is due in installments or due immediately, specify the terms)

Always ask for their payment procedure. How soon do they pay once the invoice has been submitted? Knowing this up front can alert you to early warning signs.

Get a deposit—If a job requires a deposit, send the invoice and get the deposit before you start working! If it is an hourly gig, give the invoice after a week's worth of work or whatever length of time that you feel comfortable. Do not wait too long to turn in an invoice.

Contact—Make sure you have all the proper contact information on who cuts the checks. Get their phone and fax numbers, email, and address in case you have to hunt them down!

Determine in your own mind what you will accept in the event that terms are bent. Try to have the most direct communication if terms do get changed.

Agreements—If things do get changed, do not be afraid to create a new agreement. Just be aware of what kind of leverage you have and how far you can push to get your way. There is always the chance that they will not agree, and they may find someone else. It is a fine line, but you have to be comfortable with your work conditions. Take your time in agreeing to terms the first time, before you continue to work.

NEGOTIATIONS

My wife Lisa recently had an experience that really opened her eyes. She has been an engineer for five years now and is very good. She trained under some of the most experienced engineers in music. In fact, one of her mentors was so tough on her that after this experience she finally understood why.

Lisa has been working with a very famous music legend and his multi-Grammy winning engineer for a couple years. These guys have been a successful team for over 20 years. When my wife came on board they asked me if she was good. I told them, "She is the best, but you should see for yourself!" They tried her out and the rest, as they say is history. Working with guys like these is a very special position not just because it is work, but also because it is work that is going to be noticed.

As the assistant engineer, Lisa's responsibilities were to set up microphones for tracking musicians and singers, set up outboard equipment for recording and mixing, set up the patch bay, make notes and documentation for mixes and print CDs on the Alesis Masterlink. Aside from that, she had to have the engineer's back and watch out for anything he may not see and notate anything he needed to remember. Anything that would happen in a regular commercial studio takes place in private studios as well. So the studio setting, while in someone's home studio is still very professional.

When my wife and I were expecting the birth of our first child, she let them know that she would help them find someone to fill in at the studio during her absence. When you have proven your worth and established a high level of productivity your shoes are not easy to fill.

Since Lisa is a freelance engineer she has worked in many different settings. Earlier that year she did some PA (production assistant) work on one of the popular game shows that tapes in LA. While she was working she happened to run into an old audio school classmate working at an adjacent film stage. They talked and exchanged phone numbers and emails. As they spoke, her classmate told Lisa stories about working all over LA in all sorts of audio settings. He told Lisa that he had heard that she was here and had been recording. He even knew she had worked on several Grammy-nominated projects.

Thinking to herself that this person had trained in the same program that she had, my wife asked if he would be interested in filling in while she was on maternity leave. They met at the studio and Lisa introduced him to the client. She went on to explain that the position paid $20 per hour and that the workdays for sessions ranged from six to twelve hours. She also gave a full training on what goes on in the studio and the most important pieces of equipment to learn in order to be as helpful as possible in the role of assistant. I remember her saying to her classmate, "Whatever you do, learn the Masterlink because it is used a lot."

Here is the setting:
- Assistant engineer
- Experienced high profile situation
- Credit on major productions
- $20 per hour
- Referral from classmate

If you were new to a city and you had studied audio recording and production in hopes of a career in that field, would you look at this situation as an opportunity or as just another job? In case you paused, this is a great opportunity! At a beginning level, you will be taking gigs ranging from sidecar seats to driver seats. However, in the assistant gigs, you get the chance to learn by looking over the first's shoulders and get a hands-on view of the professional process.

After a tour of the studio and a synopsis of responsibilities as well as locations of key equipment, she left the new assistant and the producer to talk. After the first meeting at the producer's suggestion it was decided that it would be best to try out the new assistant over three days to see if everyone was comfortable.

Here is where the story takes a left turn. We have a person with the desire to be in the business getting to walk in on Grammy-level activity, and all they have to do is be 100 percent into assisting and the gig is theirs. No intense paperwork, no hassle—just walk to the head of the line and step in. I should mention that the production schedule was a steady twenty to thirty hours a week for three or four months.

To make a long story short, this assistant turned into the newbie from hell. On top of not even learning the Masterlink, he crafted and asked the producer to sign a contract that would constitute an employment contract. On this contract the newbie demanded $35 per hour, $1,000 per week, overtime, and time and a half on Sundays. This was before they even made it past the three-day trial.

Needless to say, the newbie was not asked back after the three days. The reasons for non-hire were many. On top of the demands, the producer did not even like the vibe the person put off. The client sat back and wondered, what part of "Twenty dollars per hour and we work unpredictable hours" did the person not understand? Also, the first engineer had to waste time training the new person. However, the newbie didn't learn very easily, so the first engineer ended up doing the work himself. They were less than impressed!

Hint: Always meet situations with equal energy. What that means is if you are referred like that and have the first crack at the job, get to work and show your worth. You only get one chance. In addition, if you are told what an assistant's position pays never demand what you want, that information was never asked for. You can ask for the possibility for an increase, but if it is not in the budget, do not press the subject—especially if you have not even proven you are worth the extra money.

If there is no wiggle room on the rate, take the job or leave it, but make the decision one way or another. Decide if the job is worth doing at a lower rate. Ask yourself, are there other benefits? Will you get album credit? Do not wait until after the fact to make changes to the terms you previously agreed to.

Do not: verbally or through e-mails try to steer the situation into a template that you lay over every potential work situation. While the newbie rushed to secure a contract on a three-day trial, he forgot to be good at assisting, he forgot to learn the Masterlink, and he forgot that opportunities like this do not come every day.

Securing consistent work is something even experienced producers and engineers work at daily. If you want to be at the top then act like it and expect to get tested. Twenty dollars per hour is not a bad wage for that kind of work. Album credits do count for new engineers as well as experienced ones. Relationships that you come by while in school might just be your ticket to continual work.

Finally, for all you engineers just getting out of school and armed with your form letters and boilerplate contracts, please stop trying to run everything! Nothing is guaranteed so please look at all situations through glasses fitted with long term wisdom lenses. Every situation does not call for you to unfold all that you have learned while in school. You are now in the practical application phase of the exercise. Begin to develop some personality and be able to maintain a service mindset while assisting. There is a fine line between being professional and being difficult. If you really want to be in this business you will do the work required to keep moving towards your goal.

My wife could not believe that this had happened. She apologized to the producer and now she is rethinking her outlook on referring people for work. In addition, she remembered one of her teachers named Jack Robinson, who gave them hell if they made mistakes and did not pay attention to detail. As most teachers say, "One day you will thank me." Thanks Jack!

Know and understand your position! Assistant engineers are not in the best position to negotiate, especially when they do not have extensive experience. If you feel you need to discuss a rate change make sure you are doing a great job first!

When you are in a position to name your price, take advantage. Many budgets today have virtually no room. Be very sensitive; there is a fine line between being proactive and being pushy about issues associated with your rate. Being pushy will almost always get you pushed right out the door. Understand the price range of a position and work from there. Remember when you name your own price not even priceline.com accepts all demands!

Here is another story from Lisa that more than makes the point when it comes to needing an agreement on work conditions. Sometimes even a one-page note or memo faxed to a potential client after a meeting can help keep the information clear. Even if the gig is a referral, always create terms that you are comfortable with when you are discussing money and time.

Lisa was recommended to engineer for a producer because his regular engineer had become too busy to continue. During the negotiation the producer said that he did not want to pay an hourly wage (WARNING). Instead he wanted to settle on a flat daily rate. He went on to add that normally sessions would run from six to seven hours and that she could stop if the session went on too long. Sounds simple huh?

Well as it turned out the only session that went for six hours was the first one! After the first three sessions she was paid in cash. After three more sessions she felt that she had been taken advantage of. The combination of long, unnecessary hours and ear fatigue from the extremely loud control room levels made her think about their original conversation.

At the end of the session, after the singer left, she had a talk with him. She let him know exactly how she felt and specifically what they had discussed concerning session length. Here is where written records help. After being reminded of that part of the conversation the producer denied any recollection.

Once he showed who he was with his selective amnesia, Lisa explained that she would have never taken the gig unless the terms were discussed as she remembered. She also asked when the last invoices would be paid. The response was that they would not be paid until two months later, after the company had gotten their taxes together.

She decided that money was costing way too much to make and she was done with the situation. They both agreed to disagree and the producer asked her to finish working with the artist that they were currently working on and do one more session for him. She did as requested and that was her last session.

Two months passed. The check did not show up. Lisa had to call numerous times to find out when the check would be sent. Finally, after another month, a check came in the mail. The story would have a happy ending if it ended there. The check ended up NSF (non sufficient funds) and we spent an additional three weeks hounding the producer to get the full payment with penalty charges.

These stories are in here to save you the headache of chasing after your money after your services have been rendered. While this story and others may sound comical, please remember that this is how some people choose to conduct business in the real world outside of school.

In the first story the assistant engineer was walking into a $20 per hour opportunity. All they needed was to handle the workload. A simple one-page memo of the conversation would have been fine. Instead, they responded with a counter offer and a demand for more hours. They had no respect for my wife's referral or the producer's potential work situation.

In the second story Lisa could have benefited from a simple one-page agreement on conditions, especially when discussions of flat daily rates arise. She also had the negotiation power and did not use it. She was the lead engineer; there was no assistant, which means twice the workload for a single fee. When you get referred to a job always stay alert. The fact that it is a referral is no reason to relax and not follow the steps.

Every day in business there are people walking around wearing a disguise. They hide their individual motives by dressing them up as production situations and projects. Selective memory, lies, and misdirection are the tactics that these modern day terrorists of the content building world use. Be ready and understand that your time as an independent is the most valuable thing that you have. Bad business offers us an extreme view of pattern behavior and it offers you a way to be prepared.

10

Wages and Job Opportunities

Every engineer should take the time to review the movie made about the life of pioneering engineer Tom Dowd. The movie has a very poignant line that many miss. The point is made that all those years of recording were all work for hire. Now if you think about it, we are many years removed from this engineer's plight, which means that we should now understand that choosing audio engineering as a career is going to bring us just as many financial challenges as it will technical and acoustic ones.

While we are laying it on the line let's talk about this. In this industry right now you will never get a panel full of engineers (no matter how famous) on stage to freely admit what they do or do not make in exchange for their services. That being the case, we need to look at structured figures that are already in place to find a reasonable starting point for both the engineer-in-training and the engineer with experience that are both reading this book for some ideas on how to define the proper financial return on their skills. Almost every situation that requires the committed work of an engineer also requires the clever negotiation of terms.

I will lay out several different types of jobs and review some pricing schemes. Many engineers view mixing as the only way to glory. In order to just mix for a living you, need to have started recording somewhere. Many well-known mix engineers started out doing PA for clubs and bands. Many started out in broadcast doing radio; some are now out of music and into TV and film. Whatever the path, they all evolved into the pricing that they use in a similar fashion. Unless they were fortunate to be in a union-regulated job setting, they made up their rate the best way they knew how. Early on, many engineers maintained professional relationships with producers. As the producer worked, they were gradually able to increase their rate.

Let's look at some hard figures. According to a 2007 Talent Shortage Survey, three of the ten jobs listed are applicable for our conversation. These jobs are most in need of qualified workers right now. Due to high demand, pursuing a job in one of these fields could mean increased pay and more benefits for those willing to focus on these careers. Please notice that the two-year associate's degree actually generates a higher annual salary.

I picked these three due to the fact that right now many of our engineers are going into the teaching profession. Some of the teachers in the larger private audio schools do not have a formal degree. Life experience is relevant when seeking a career as an audio educator. The other two technology-based careers are in line with most experienced audio engineers. By using these figures alongside where you are in your career you will be able to extract a relevant dollar figure that will be in line with the current trend. The number you arrive at is not an absolute but instead a starting point or goal for you to use as you target your desired wage.

Teachers
Qualifications: Educational qualifications for postsecondary teacher jobs range from expertise in a particular field to a Ph.D., depending on the subject being taught and the type of educational institution.
   Average salary: $45,281

Engineering Technicians
Qualifications: An associate's degree in engineering technology from a technical institute, vocational school or community college, creativity, and good communications skills.
   Average salary: $47,759

Technical Support Specialist

Technical support specialists ensure computer systems are working properly, address technical problems, and train workers in using computer equipment. Many of these professionals have a bachelor's degree in their field of specialty. As computer networks expand, more technical support specialists may be able to work from home.

Average salary: $63,993

These three descriptions and salary ranges can be used to target your goals and calculate your earning potential. My suggestion would be to use these as general starting points to help you possibly determine your figures. Remember that where you live, as well as your experience, all factor into your fees and opportunities.

Here are some different types of audio engineering jobs listed under the activity where you will find them. In some cases rates will vary depending upon the type of employer, private studio vs. commercial facility, or in some cases union vs. non-union work. Remember that our business and most independent situations are ruled by the "creative deal." So, when you are looking for work use this info to understand how many related areas use personnel with audio engineering skills.

Theatre Work (Live Plays, Musicals, and Special Events):
- Master Audio Engineer
- Mixing Engineer

- Sound Designer / Operator
- Audio Technician
- Stage Hand / Loaders

Live Concerts (Tours and Musical Presentations):
- Systems Engineer
- Front of House Engineer
- Monitor Engineer
- Instrument Technician
- Keyboard Technician
- Drum Technician
- Guitar Technician
- Bass Technician
- Percussion Technician

Recording:
- Chief Engineer
- Mix Engineer
- Recording Engineer
- Assistant Engineer
- Maintenance Engineer
- Voice Over Engineer
- Mastering Engineer
- Archival Engineer

Television and Film (News, Game Shows, Sitcoms, and Movies):
- Mix Engineer
- Foley Engineer

- ADR / Post
- Sound Mixer
- Boom Operator
- Utility Sound Technician
- Technical Maintenance Engineer
- Recordist (audio playback)
- Broadcast Engineer
- Master Control Operator
- Archival Engineer

Corporate:
- Audio and Sound Design for Video Games
- Audio Test Engineer (Q /A)
- Research and Development
- Pro Audio Sales
- Corporate Audio Visual Specialist
- Theme Park Audio Specialist
- Theme Park Mix Engineer
- Cruise Ship Audio Specialist
- Cruise Ship Audio Engineer

Church Audio:
- Audio/Visual Department
- Front of House Engineer
- Monitor Engineer
- Duplication Engineer

Law Enforcement:
- Forensic Audio
- Audio Criminalist

Independent:
- Home Theatre Technician
- Studio Consultant
- Studio Maintenance Technician
- Studio Wiring Technician

Please remember that the job opportunities listed cover the major areas where you can apply your skills as an audio engineer as well as any other professional certifications and experience that you have acquired along your journey as a professional.

In the last five years this profession has many times resembled the Wild West during the gold rush days. Many want to come in quick and get all the gold lying on the ground. On the other hand, some of us engineers have been prospecting for years. We recognize when it is time to dig and when it is time to keep looking. It is because of the sheer increase in the number of engineers now available that pricing will never be confined to one specific table. It is really determined situation by situation.

We all have heard the advice to "Start at the bottom and empty trash cans." While the bottom-to-the-top method is the way many interns start, more and more people are looking at audio for a career choice. Let's look at some alternative methods of getting where you want to be. I have some short descriptions that are taken from real careers of engineers who are working today. These are the actual ways that have worked for them.

CASE #1 THE GUY NEXT TO THE GUY

Many engineers, including me, started out in manufacturing. The development of musical electronic products has led many of us to step away from our roles as company product specialists and directly into strategic engineering positions. Working on new products requires a different set of skills. It also makes you very quick because you are working with the tools all the time. Many guys who now work on big projects got their break because they are quick at what they do. They did not necessarily have a well of recording experience. They have used their technical knowledge to create their opportunities. For me, being able to understand all electronic music products down to a component level was the key to remaining in the room to participate in other activity.

Whenever an artist or record exec/producer is contacted, she or he has a team of people she or he trusts to give them the results that keep both projects and money coming in the door. The "in house" engineer who is able to be on a production team and give total project allegiance can find a comfortable position with a consistent paycheck that may vary depending on budget. That person usually gets paid on a per project basis and has a schedule of activity that is several months ahead. Fees can range from $25 to $65 per hour, all the way to $500 per song and sometimes more. I call this "the guy next to the guy" because that is when your skills get you right next to the guy who calls the shots.

CASE #2 THE ASSISTANT

The assistant engineer is very important in the job spectrum and cannot be overlooked or undervalued. However, assistants usually make a starting wage of $15-25 per hour. Successful navigation of this job position can help set the stage for your own opportunity later on. Right now in this day and age you are only as strong as your database. Working at an assistant level allows you to view successful business relationships in progress. You can build your own connections by being a productive team member. Eventually assistants have to step out and test their lessons learned. If done correctly, they can sometimes test the water by handling the overflow work that their efficient assisting has created. This position allows you to observe the successful behavior that you will need when it is your turn to move up. Always keep a level head and no matter how much you learn in school, never ever abandon your common sense.

CASE #3 THE ENGINEER WITH REPRESENTATION

This engineer has a company or person who acts as a booking agent/manager, and navigates the politics of the business in order to secure work for their clients. Many engineers who focus on mixing use this method. The agent or handler gets a percentage of the negotiated fee. This is a great method once you have some hits under your belt, but it is a very costly thing to have a manager.

While you are glad to have the work, you might eventually realize that you are working for them instead of them working for you!

Mixing a record is a skill, a practiced craft. Playing politics and negotiating work opportunities are strategies or tactics—that is the difference. When this trend started we had several companies claiming to be the best at getting their herd of engineers work. Unfortunately this strategy backfired as more work went to the engineers who gave the biggest percentage to the handlers. Look at that. Politics to navigate the politics of securing work.

Growth is great, but before you take on the cost of a handler or agent do all you can to educate yourself about where your dollars are and the many roads to them. Take your time to figure out what you want out of a manager's services.

CASE # 4 THE ENGINEER WITH GEAR

More and more you will find that many engineers in both live sound and studio settings will have their own high-priced equipment. This self-sufficiency is another way to create your own door directly to clientele. I saw the trend start in pro sound for tours. Many sound rental companies want to guarantee that they get in on tour situations so they seek out the most popular sound engineers, monitor engineers, etc. and they sponsor them with the use of a console.

That guarantees that the engineer can say to the artist, "I will give you my price for weekly service and by the way I have my own console." Once the engineer is in place he can then specify his preference for the sound company when that selection is being made. It happens all the time and it is just business people using relationships.

This style has not gone unnoticed. Many recording engineers now have their own large-format consoles, portable mobile studios, and other custom high-end equipment. The exclusivity that these key hardware purchases makes is also a good way to create your own door that opens directly to new clients and consistent work. Mobile recording is something that can give you the edge as well. Learning to capture original content in the field will challenge every aspect of engineering skill and knowledge that you have within you.

A good friend of mine is an Emmy-winning engineer and while he started out mixing music, he found his niche by developing a very exclusive but effective audio playback system for TV and live music presentations. While he still mixes two popular shows, his system is also for rent. So when a TV special is being taped and they need to play back tracks for musical performances, they call him to rent his gear. His system is so unique that there are not many like it out there, so his price for the rental includes his fee as the operator. The client pays one price and gets an award-winning engineer along with the rental of the specialized gear.

CASE #5 THE ENGINEER BY DEFAULT

This is an occurrence that arose with the introduction of the Tascam Portastudio. Many composers, musicians, and songwriters all claim to be engineers now. I am not saying that it cannot be done. But let's look at the trend closely. If you have to do a function out of necessity rather than intention, that makes a big difference on how you look at the process.

Composers, musicians, and songwriters all create the content. However, the engineer's specific role has always been to capture and document the creative effort. While they may know what they hear in their heads, a skilled audio engineer who intended to do just what they do knows how to complement what they do by focusing on the capture and mix process. It seems simple but because the tools of creation are now so readily available, we have many engineers by default.

This road to work is fine. However, I can warn you when you commit to working on a client's project it helps to not have other things pulling at you. You need to be committed to everything that you say you are working on. Your own unfulfilled desires as a musician or superstar must not interfere. When you are selling your engineering skills, please remember, do not force feed your musical chops into the situation until it is asked for. I have witnessed many guys early on lose opportunities because they did the, "I'm an engineer who can play every part on your record" dance. Eventually, the project becomes the vision of the dominating musician/engineer and it is out of the hands of its originator.

It is very interesting that many songwriters/producers now secure the ability to assign engineering duties as part of their deal. Music is not a hustle! Audio engineering work and the billable time associated with it should never be taken lightly. If you have a producer that you work with, great! But, always try to negotiate your own rates. I have seen this particular method backfire because the producer has the in for the work, but actually starts to take notice of the engineer's rates. Then, he begins to cut into the engineering wage to find the profit in a job that was underbid from the start. The control that you give up when going for the "hook up" can be a risky gamble.

For many years I have been able to be of service to many musicians and producers. The main reason for my consistency is that I never wanted to be the people that I worked with. If you are a musician who is an engineer by default, consider having some key relationships with committed engineers. It will change how you create to let an engineer work with you. It will give you a set of checks and balances. It is money well spent to find good engineers to work with. Whatever your approach to securing work, always remember that intention determines the outcome.

OTHER AREAS FOR EMPLOYMENT

Archiving: for companies, individuals, and special organizations. This is still an area where you can find lots of work. Tape vaults and cold storage locations offer many ways to use your knowledge of converting analog tapes to digital files. The tapes of the past are the birthplaces for content of the future.

Many producers spend time in the archives of publishing companies' tape vaults. I saw this a lot in jazz music. Producers look through and assemble many compilation-type projects based on these expeditions. They understand that projects come in all forms even if you never worked with someone historic. To re-purpose, re-mix, or just build a compilation disc based on previously recorded material is the same as actually having worked with that person.

Most of those producers gained access to the archives through the politics of the business. Since the content usually belongs to someone, help them make some money and you might create your opportunity.

Specialized Audio: Government contracts and private corporations. The UN, UNESCO and other large organizations have the need for audio engineers and technical support. They use simultaneous translation/ recording systems. They have special functions weekly and use live PA.

A friend of mine is a mix engineer and just got the contract to mix the Air Force Band's jazz record. In addition, many corporations such as Apple, Microsoft, and IBM employ their own internal audio/video personnel.

Theatre: Multi-media playback for plays, live sound mixer for musicals and other stage performances, sound designing for stage plays, and corporate presentations. Sometimes these positions are actual employment with the city that the venue or venues are in. City positions for sound engineers are usually tiered according to how long each audio person has been there as well as their skill level.

Church and Worship: Most churches have multiple services as well as special events, picnics, etc. In small churches, volunteers usually staff the audio department. In larger churches and those increasing in membership, the audio department has paid positions. While it may not be live touring, it is audio engineering work. No matter what the faith, they use technology. It is a venue like any other place with lights and a stage that has a specific worship component in the midst of all the other audio/visual activity. This setting has the need for competent live engineers as well as postproduction audio specialists.

Audio for Video, Film, and TV: Many shows, especially in local news and entertainment markets, are shot and produced by small groups of people. Among them is the live sound engineer. In this case he is responsible for ENG (Electronic News Gathering). The audio engineer in the field is responsible for capturing and mixing audio to camera. Shows like EXTRA, Entertainment Tonight, and the News all need audio professionals to ensure the quality of their audio before it gets to the studio.

Audio Production for the Video Game Industry: This is one of the more popular areas that have sprung up in the past ten years. This particular specialization allows many engineers who also have musical abilities to work by themselves for maximum financial gain. It is composing for interactive media and involves not only music but dialog as well as original sound effects.

Forensic Audio: with the popularity of the CSI-based crime shows we have seen the rise in the exposure of yet another longstanding but not as well known career in audio. What in the past was referred to as the court-appointed audio expert, now goes by the professional title of Forensic Audio Specialist. This person uses their skills to listen to audio recordings and determine if there is any evidentiary value present. Since I am in Los Angeles, one of the most knowledgeable guys out there is longtime industry veteran Wes Dooley and his company Audio Engineering Associates. I met him in a store early on in my training. I was amazed at how he took the whole experience of using a microphone and let me know some history behind what was going on. He shared knowledge about microphones and audio because it is his passion. Since then he has expanded his service to include forensic audio/video examination, as well as authentication and recreation for court proceedings. In addition, he also makes high-quality microphones. He is an award-winning engineer, forty-plus years into his career and he has diversified enough to actually steer his career where most would not. Please visit his Website at: (www.wesdooley.com)

PROPOSAL AND BUDGET WRITING

Proposals are the basis for the rules of engagement in business. They help to make the basic direction of a project clear. When you back up and look at the complete picture it's easy to see that in order to end up in "agreement," you must first propose something to agree on. Proposals are needed for:

- Original ideas
- Studio design
- Consultations
- Any job you are competing for with other contactors/engineers
- Grants and special funding

If you meet with a potential client about an upcoming project, a written proposal might be the deciding factor in whether or not you get the job. Do not assume that just talking about a project will help you get the job. Go the extra mile and write a proposal! That paper and pen we talked about earlier is a sign of respect. Put them to use when you meet with your client and take notes on the important facts of the meeting. Pay close attention to deadline dates, key words, and names of responsible people that you will have to interface with.

Your writing skills and the ability to communicate will be exposed in your letters and proposals. Pay attention to your language, grammar, spelling, and punctuation. You are trying to persuade the potential client to actually do what you are proposing. If you look bad on paper, it can hurt your image and affect your chance at the gig. Typos and errors imply that you are either stupid or that you didn't bother to take the time to make sure that everything was correct. Even if that's not true, it is still distracting to the reader.

I make it a habit to write a letter three times. The first time is to dump all my thoughts. The second version is to edit down the letter so that it only includes the most important facts. The final time is to make sure I can say the most with the fewest words. By taking my time, I can say exactly what I need to in order to be as effective as possible.

Remember, you are a walking business. You have to present yourself well in person, on the phone, and on paper. This business is built on reputations and referrals. Your ability to craft effective communications could be the key factor that helps you get a shot.

Rather than giving you a form letter to copy I am going to show you two different ways to write a letter. The first way is kind and sincere and uses no affirmative language. The second way is effective with specific language and uses a technique called "the assumptive close."

Example 1:

Dear Mr. Brown,

It was a pleasure meeting with you today. I hope that we can find a way to work together on your company's project. I would like to get together when you get some time and discuss some of my ideas.

Sincerely,
Mr. Hopes A. Lot

Example 2:

Dear Mr. Brown,

Thank you for taking the time to meet today. I know that we can provide the services that your company needs. If your schedule allows I would like to meet next week to discuss our solutions and target a start date for work to begin.

Thanks again for your time,
Knockingitout D. Park

In Example 1, the author of the letter has hopes. He was just in a meeting with a company in need of service. Either he can do the work or he can't! Waiting until an executive has time to respond gives him room to not call you back at all. Also, when you say something like, "my ideas" it makes you appear self-serving and more focused on credit than conveying your company's strength as a team.

In Example 2, the author knows and is sure he can do the required work from the first sentence. In the second sentence, he is respecting the executives schedule but moving directly into an assumptive close. Assumptive closes never give the reader a chance to really say no. To say no in this case would mean Mr. Brown would be turning his back on his company needs, solutions, and start dates to work.

Both of these examples are basic, but you get the point. When you write letters, e-mails and have conversations, be sure not to be full of "hopes." Always be firm on dates and times. Finally, always thank people for their time.

Form letters are great as a starting point but think about who you are writing to. Be sincere. In business, trust is what is bought and sold most often. If you are going to use form letters then take the time to personalize them to fit, and whenever possible put some of your style and personality in everything you do, even writing letters!

Here is where your basic writing skill set comes into play. By taking notes, I have found over the years that it is important to notate how your client says something in addition to what is actually said. I have seen many people cut their opportunities short because they were not into their clients' needs. Instead, they were doing everything for the money. They felt no need to "read the room" as we say.

Proposal Format:

There are several items in a proposal that I consider key elements for showing good business sense and landing a client. Begin with a cover letter that includes:

- Your company letterhead (Microsoft Word has templates)
- Client info
- Greetings, refer to conversations or previous meetings
- Explain what is included in your proposal.
- Layout your involvement in the project, with delivery of product specifications.
- Your fee with deposit and balance due info
- End the letter with an "assumptive close" (but don't be pushy!).
- Follow the cover letter with additional info: budget and any other project specs.

I have included an altered copy of one of my agreements. Check it out and see how the details provided by the client are used to create clearly defined solutions. Look for a version of the assumptive close in the writing style.

> # Company Name

Date
Recipient Name
Title
Company Name
Primary Business Address
City, XX Zipcode

Dear Mr. X,

Thank you for meeting with us. It is a pleasure to be working together to create the new Good Lord Community Church! The following figures outline our involvement as consultants on the proposed Phase I—Kids World. Our company understands that this project has two major phases, with July 1st being the deadline for Phase I.

The audio/video consulting services of (Your Company Name) will include delivering the specified list of A/V equipment (with cut sheets for the electrician), and any other suggestions with Phase II in mind. Below you will find a breakdown of the meeting information that we got from you. We will be using this to create the Audio/Visual specification for this project.

The fee to consult on Phase 1 is $$$. A deposit of (half) $$$ is due before we start assembling the information enclosed. The balance is due upon the delivery of the paperwork, on or before the date of the July 1st submission deadline.

Breakdown of Meeting:
• Locations for all low voltage connectivity (phone, fax, computers, etc.)

- Phone/voice mail system as well as all administration communication needs for daycare.
- Security system tie-in.
- Camera type as well as placement, and other specialty wiring needed for security of daycare area.
- Placement, type of specialty keypads and special access door hardware for daycare area.
- 70-volt paging system designed for daycare as an emergency evacuation system. (Note: This system is expandable to work with the growth of the facility.) Audio system for daycare that includes: CD player, DVD audio, iPod and other forms of playback, small audio mixer and microphones with professional speakers placed in four corners for even spread of sound.
- A video system will be designed for the daycare. It will include a drop-down screen, a fixed projector, and a portable display unit. Feed from both the cable company and the satellite company.
- All wires will be home run to a location on the first floor next to the electrical panel for the facility.
- For Phase 1, the low voltage wiring closet will be required to have future conduit stubs that will feed into the second floor area. (Note: Other conduit stubs will be required for church growth.)
- For Phase 1, the main computer/server for the Daycare will be housed in the Administrator's office and relocated later.

Thanks again for choosing to work with (Your Company Name) for consultation on your expansion project.

Sincerely,
Dave Hampton
President, MATK Corp.

When I started to do consultations I did work at a lot of local churches. I remember running into a certain professional sound engineer. I knew him as a live engineer. I did not know he had done church work as well. I found myself getting called to a very well known church in the inner city. They had contracted him to design and install a new system but all he had done was get them two speakers and a couple of pieces of new gear. Needless to say, they were not happy.

After reviewing the facility, I gave them my cost for coming in behind a bad job to create a working system for Sunday's service. I drew up an agreement and started. I re-wired the main mix position as well as cleaned up the A/C wires and audio cables. I kept looking at the custom speakers that this guy had built for the church and knew something was not right.

I finally got up on a ladder and removed the speaker and disassembled it. It turned out that the engineer went to great lengths to have the speaker boxes made to match the wooden church pews. However, the problem was that he filled the boxes with cheap speaker components. I got it working and sounding great and went on Sunday to oversee the first service and make sure the client was pleased.

I use this story to illustrate several points:

1. It pays to understand what you are walking into. A consultation on a brand new job, rather than on a

messed up one, means that you are starting with a client in a good mood. A client who feels that they have been ripped off is sometimes frantic at the first meeting and many times is hesitant at trusting you right away.

2. Always include enough money to cover extra costs on jobs where you are coming in after the fact.

3. Follow up your emergency calls with a personal visit. It shows that you care about your clients and your work.

4. Always read the non-verbal cues in the room. In this case, I was sensitive to the fact that the pastor who is the leader of his congregation felt bad because the previous contractor had taken advantage of his kindness. When a church makes a purchase, the whole church makes it. The monies come from every member. Being accountable is an absolute for doing any type of contracting, especially churches.

BUDGETS

An important tip to remember when dealing with budgets is to only give details when necessary. When I first started, I was very wordy with proposals, invoices, and budgets. I found that many clients prefer to get the big picture (final cost) in view. Many clients only need to know your hourly rate and final charge. The details are actually more for you as the independent contractor.

When I'm asked for a budget, I generally work in round numbers. It really helps for special projects to plan the budget around what services your client needs, as well as any other information such as cost restrictions. An example of this for our industry would be a client who needs an engineer to mix and master his project. Many engineers are choosing to offer this service now. I would suggest that you consult your local mastering house and ask their rate per song. That fee combined with your regular mix fee will be fair and you will not be "giving away the farm."

On specialized audio projects such as church audio you might consider looking at the facts surrounding the project. I consulted for a pastor whose ministry was expanding and building a new church. They wanted key audio information on a job that was scheduled for completion in ten months.

Here is the challenge. To give definitive costs on an installation that is over six months away means that I need to factor in the possibility of newer technology and the cost changes associated with that. Every time you make a budget it will be dependent on the situation. As long as you follow a format that helps your client understand what they are paying for it will be fine. You should also ask your client how they like to see the budgets. If they don't have a preference, that leaves you a direct path to layout the budget however you like. Always ask as many questions as you can. Remember that Budgets + Approval = Checks.

Here is a list of tips regarding budget items:

Budget Format:

- The budget should be easy to read at a very quick glance.
- Break it down to subcategories so it flows.
- Make totals bold print so there is no confusion.
- If you don't format your budget in a table, make sure the spacing makes sense.
- Be sure to explain labor fees in the letter: how many hours will be spent on the project and how many people it includes.

The following page shows a section of a budget that follows the format discussed. Please look at all the details and how they can easily be understood because they are laid out properly. The sample budget is for a small live concert computer support system.

I hope that sharing this information with you will help you land more gigs and improve your reputation in the industry.

Budget for System

Hardware & Assembly	Cost
Computer	$3,000.00
Accessories	$1,600.00
System Case	$1,000.00
Wiring	$750.00
Software	$1,400.00
Studio Time	$2,500.00
TOTAL	$10,250.00
Design, Programming, & Assembly	$8,500 per week
(Project time = 4 weeks) Total	$34,000.00
System Total	$44,250.00

- Deposit to start will be the hardware cost plus first week's pay.
  - ✶ The deposit is $18,750.00
- Payment of weekly work fee will be every Friday from start of project.
  - ✶ The weekly payment is $ 8,500.00

Independent Contracting Versus Corporate Employment

WHAT IS THE DIFFERENCE?

Although earlier in my career I had a corporate gig, I wanted to get these answers from someone who is currently working in corporate America. I contacted my friend Dirk Scirotta, Emmy award-winning TV mixing engineer. This is what we talked about.

Dave Hampton: I have a theory that things are different out there (on all levels) when you are an independent audio engineer dealing with clients versus being employed by a company. Working in corporate employment as an audio engineer dealing with a boss and clients, do you agree/disagree with this theory?

Dirk Scirotta: Sure, but the bottom line is you are being paid to do what *the client* wants you to do. Either way you are an audio puppet in some way. In one way there is a client telling a boss telling you what to do. The other way is you are just doing what the client is telling you to do. Also, the boss will need to make money, so you will probably make less that way.

DH: What is it like working in corporate America today?

DS: To me it depends on what you need out of it. I personally need to support my family, so I am happy to be busy. If I had no family to support and I was simply some hotshot mixer in the business, I would probably hate it. Sounds weird, but makes sense to me.

DH: As an audio engineer is there a different mindset between the two environments?

DS: I don't think so. We are engineers and what we do is engineer no matter who is paying us. There will always be an end product either way.

DH: Can you compare the two environments?

DS: Honestly, I can only think of money and communication. It's much nicer to deal with the clients directly and cut out all that middleman crap that just slows down a project.

DH: Has the ever-evolving music industry affected the rest of corporate America as far as audio engineering goes?

DS: I think audio engineers are just like any other employee doing anything out there. There is someone paying us for our work so we do what they want. If corporate America changes, audio engineers have to change.

DH: Are jobs sparse or overflowing for audio engineers in corporate America?

DS: That is a subjective question. In my world, audio engineering is a "skilled labor" position. There are also many levels of "profile" for the work being done. High profile down to very low profile could be the difference in budgets or quality of an artist or simply the untrained ear dealing with the business aspect instead of the product being made. I would not say sparse, but in TV world, there are very few working in the high-profile venues in broadcast engineering, and they are kept very busy.

DH: If you take independent gigs on the side, mentally what do you go through when you are making a transition from going to your corporate gig to an independent gig?

DS: I am still engineering and that is that no matter who it is for. They pay me, I work. However, I do constantly battle with loyalty. One client might have a full nine months of work for me and another may only have a week. In this case I would be more loyal to the 9-month client and give them the first chance to book me. I would not screw a 9-month client to satisfy a week of work.

DH: Which do you like better?

DS: Independent, of course. You can focus more on your skill rather than the lack of communication while getting to the skill portion of your job.

DH: How do colleagues act in a corporate setting? Is it a cutthroat environment?

DS: I personally have not had a problem with cutthroat colleagues. In the field I currently work in it is more of a family than anything. There is enough work for all of us and we are always helping each other out, covering for one another, teaching one another, and so on. Like I said before, there are not a lot of people doing what I am doing around here.

DH: How is the upward movement of promotion in your environment?

DS: Very well, if you show promise. Skill is a large portion and your work ethic is another. You can always strive for a higher position if you want it. This is true in any environment.

DH: What would someone new to audio be surprised to know about working in corporate America?

DS: Someone new would be surprised to see how everyone knows everyone. You can't get away from it. You do one job and everyone in the "family" will know how you did. That will determine your next gig.

DH: What's the best way to go about getting a corporate gig? What is impressive to see on a résumé? How should someone treat their interview?

DS: Not really a valid question I could answer. I have never submitted a résumé or suffered through an interview. But, what you can do is be easygoing, stress free, and good at what you do. Don't talk bullshit or gossip about bullshit. Give the impression of knowing where you are and what you're supposed to do at all times. Even if you don't know what to do, you can ask, but you can also give the feeling of confidence at the same time. Don't get me wrong here, do not claim you can do something if you can't. That's never good.

DH: What type of person fits into a corporate gig? What does it take to succeed at a corporate gig as an engineer?

DS: Easy communication skills and personality. You need to get along with *many* types of people in a high stress field. Oh, yeah, skill too!

I thought this interview would be helpful because Dirk has worked in both union and non-union situations as well as studio recording and live sound. He has successfully navigated his career to be able to work in many different audio environments.

12

Legally Forming Your Own Company

WHEN YOU ARE READY TO MAKE THE PLUNGE

When it comes to business, never be afraid to ask questions. Do research into how others in the business run their professional lives. I worked for fifteen years under a DBA (Doing Business As), and did not incorporate until 2000. DBA states that you are doing business under a company name. It is the most basic form of establishing a business identity. On the other hand, my wife incorporated while still in school. Once she graduated, she already knew how to apply big business models to her first small studio. She skipped over at least nine years of unusual situations by setting up a business model correctly from the start.

Everyone entering her studio doors was using the facility as well as her expertise. They came to her; she did not go pick them up. I say these things to illustrate to you how even on a small studio level, big preparatory steps help ensure that clients get what they come for: Results! And that you get what you are in business for: to get paid!

BENEFITS OF FORMING A CORPORATION

Whether you are just starting your business or you have already been operating a business as a sole proprietorship or general partnership, you may be wondering about the benefits of forming your business as a corporation. Often business owners think that incorporation is too costly or too time-consuming, and neither is the case.

The benefits the owners gain by forming their business as a corporation typically outweigh any perceived disadvantages. These benefits are, in many cases, unavailable to sole proprietorships and general partnerships. As an audio engineer you are an independent contractor. Put simply you are the company and the sooner you realize and establish that, the better off you will be. If you have a structured position as an in-house audio engineer then you are fortunate to have a steady nine-to-five job with a consistent check and hopefully a benefit package. If, however, you are an engineer who goes from job to job doing work for hire then you need to take some notes. Incorporation benefits include:

- **Limited Liability**—Corporations provide limited liability protection to their owners (who are called shareholders). Typically, the owners are not personally responsible for the debts and liabilities of the business; thus, creditors cannot pursue owners' personal assets, such as a house or car, to pay business debts. Conversely, in a sole proprietorship or general partnership, owners and the business are legally considered the same and personal assets can be used to pay business debts.

- **Tax Advantages**—Corporations often gain tax advantages, such as the deductibility of health insurance premiums paid on behalf of an owner-employee; savings on self-employment taxes, as corporate income is not subject to Social Security, Workers Compensation and Medicare taxes; and the deductibility of other expenses such as life insurance. For information on the types of tax advantages your business may gain by forming as a corporation, please speak with an accountant or tax advisor.

- **Establishing Credibility**—Incorporating may help a new business establish credibility with potential customers, employees, vendors and partners.

- **Unlimited Life**—A corporation's life is not dependent upon its owners. A corporation possesses the feature of unlimited life, meaning if an owner dies or wishes to sell his or her interest, the corporation will continue to exist and do business.

- **Transferability of Ownership**—Ownership in a corporation is typically easily transferable. (However, there are restrictions on S corporation ownership.)

- **Raising Capital**—Capital can be raised more easily through the sale of stock. Additionally, many banks, when providing a small business loan, want the borrower to be an incorporated business.

- **Retirement plans**—Retirement funds and qualified retirements plans, such as a 401(k), may be established more easily.

CORPORATIONS DO NOT COME WITHOUT PERCEIVED POTENTIAL DISADVANTAGES.

Potential disadvantages of a corporation include:

- **Double Taxation**—C corporations are subject to double taxation of corporate profits when corporate income is distributed to the owners in the form of dividends. The double tax is created when tax is first paid at the corporate level. If corporate profit is then distributed to owners as dividends, the owners pay tax at the individual level on that income. The double tax can be avoided by electing S corporation tax status with the Internal Revenue Service.

- **Formation and Ongoing Expenses**—To form a corporation, articles of incorporation must be filed with the state and the applicable state filing fees paid. Many states impose ongoing fees on corporations, such as annual report and/or franchise tax fees. While these fees often are not very expensive for small businesses, formation of a corporation is more expensive than for a sole proprietorship or general partnership, both of which are not required to file formation documents with the state.

- **Corporate formalities**—Corporations are required to follow both initial and annual record-keeping tasks, such as holding and properly documenting initial and annual meetings of directors and shareholders, adopting and maintaining bylaws and issuing shares of stock to the owners. Sole proprietorships, general partnerships and even LLCs do not incur the formalities imposed on corporations.

C CORPORATIONS VERSUS S CORPORATIONS

When entrepreneurs consider starting a business, or when existing small business owners consider changing their business structure, one of the most common options they evaluate is the corporation. There are two different types of corporations, the C corporation and the S corporation, and which is best often depends on the goals you have for your business.

The C corporation is the standard corporation. The S corporation is a standard corporation that has elected a special tax status with the Internal Revenue Service (IRS). It gets its name because it is defined in Subchapter S of the Internal Revenue Code. In order to elect S corporation status, Form 2553 must be filed with the IRS and all S corporation guidelines met.

While the C corporation and S corporation have many similarities, they also have distinct differences.

Similarities

- Both offer the same limited liability protection for shareholders (owners), meaning that the shareholders are typically not personally responsible for the debts and liabilities of the business.

- Both are separate legal entities created by a state filing.

- The formation documents that are filed with the state, which are typically called the articles of incorporation or certificate of incorporation, are the same whether the business will be a C or an S corporation.

- Corporations have shareholders, directors, and officers. Shareholders are the owners of the company and elect the board of directors. The board of directors oversees and directs the affairs of the corporation and has responsibility for major decisions, but is not responsible for the day-to-day operations of the corporation. The directors elect officers to manage the daily affairs of the business. Most states allow one person be a shareholder, director, and officer of a corporation.

- Both are required to follow the same internal and external corporate formalities. Examples of internal formalities include adopting bylaws, issuing stock, holding initial and then annual meetings of shareholders and directors, and keeping the minutes from these meetings with the corporate records. Examples of external requirements include filing annual reports, which are required by the state, and paying the necessary annual fees.

Differences

1. Taxation
- C corporations are separately taxable entities. C corporations file a corporate tax return reporting profits or losses, and any profits are taxed at the

corporate level. C corporations face the possibility of double taxation when profits are distributed to shareholders in the form of dividends, as the shareholders must report dividends as personal income and pay tax on them at the individual level.

- S corporations are pass-through tax entities. Pass-through taxation is discussed more below.

2. Corporate ownership

- C corporations can have an unlimited number of shareholders, while S corporations are restricted to no more than 100 shareholders.

- C corporations can have non-US residents as shareholders, but S corporations cannot.

- S corporations cannot be owned by C corporations, other S corporations, LLCs, partnerships, or many trusts. C corporations are not subject to these same restrictions.

- S corporations can have only one class of stock (disregarding voting rights). C corporations can have multiple classes of stock.

3. S corporation election

- S corporations must make a timely filing of Form 2553 with the IRS. The IRS instructions indicate this form must be completed and filed:

- At any time before the sixteenthth day of the third month of the tax year the election is to take effect, or

- At any time during the tax year preceding the tax year it is to take effect.

- An election made no later than two months and fifteen days after the beginning of a tax year that is less than two-and-a-half months long is treated as timely for that year.

- An election made after the fifteenth day of the third month but before the end of the tax year generally is effective for the next tax year. However, an election made after the fifteenthth day of the third month will be accepted as timely filed if the corporation can show that failure to file on time was due to reasonable cause.

Pass-through Taxation

As mentioned above, electing S corporation status with the IRS allows for pass-through taxation of the corporation's profits. S corporations must still file corporate tax returns, but they do not pay taxes at the corporate level. The corporation's profits are passed-through to the individual tax returns of the shareholders, and taxes are paid on those profits at the individual tax rate. If the corporation is reporting a loss, the loss is passed-through to the shareholders as well. Because S corporations do not pay taxes at the corporate level, this eliminates the potential double tax C corporations face when profits are issued as dividends to shareholders.

FORMING AN S CORPORATION

An S corporation is a standard corporation that has elected a special tax status with the Internal Revenue Service (IRS). The formation requirements for an S corporation are the same as those for a C corporation, wherein formation documents must be filed with the appropriate state agency and the necessary state filing fees paid. This is probably the most logical type of corporation for an independent audio engineer.

One reason so many small business owners choose to elect S corporation status with the IRS is that the S corporation's special tax status eliminates the possibility of double taxation common to C corporations. With S corporations, a corporate income tax return is filed but no tax is paid at the entity level. Instead, the profits or losses of the corporation are "passed-through" to the shareholders and are reported on their individual tax returns.

Advantages of an S Corporation:

- S corporations avoid the possibility of double taxation on profits

- Shareholders of an S corporation are typically not personally responsible for the debts and liabilities of the business

- Ownership of an S corporation is easily transferable through the sale of stock

- S corporations have unlimited life extending beyond the illness or death of the owners

- Additional capital can be raised by selling shares of the S corporation's stock

- Potential customers may perceive an S corporation as a more professional entity than a sole proprietorship or partnership

- S corporations are generally audited less frequently than sole proprietorships

- Certain S corporation business expenses may be tax-deductible

- S corporations can result in self-employment tax savings

- S corporations may provide a number of income and tax savings

S corporations are subject to restrictions imposed by the IRS on who can be owners. S corporation owners (shareholders) must meet the following criteria:

- Number fewer than 100
- Cannot be non-resident aliens
- Cannot be C corporations, other S corporations, limited liability companies (LLCs), partnerships or certain trusts.

To create an S corporation, the proper formation documents, typically called the articles of incorporation or certificate of incorporation, must be filed with the appropriate state agency and the necessary state filing fees paid. After the corporation is created at the state level, a timely filing of the IRS Form 2553 is necessary to elect S corporation status. The election process takes approximately sixty days, according to the IRS instructions.

INFORMATION FREQUENTLY REQUIRED ON INCORPORATION DOCUMENTS

If you are considering forming your business as a corporation, one question you may have is, "What information is required on the incorporation documents?" Knowing this ahead of time will save time as you begin the incorporation process.

The formation document for a corporation is called the "articles of incorporation" or "certificate of incorporation."

Each state has its own version of this document creating a number of variances in the amount and type of information required. This article outlines the most common information requested by the states.

- Company Name—The desired name of the corporation must be included. That name must typically contain a corporate identifier, such as "Corporation," "Incorporated," "Company," or an abbreviation of those terms, such as "Inc." Undertaking a preliminary name availability search prior to submitting the articles of incorporation will help to see if your desired name is available. Keep in mind that the state holds final approval rights on the desired name to ensure it is not already in use by another company in that state or is not "deceptively similar" to a name already in use.

- Business Purpose—The business purpose is an explanation of what the company is formed to do or provide. There are two types of business purpose clauses: general and specific.

- General business purpose—some states will accept a general-purpose clause, which basically states that the company is formed to engage in "all lawful business."

- Specific business purpose—some states require a more detailed explanation of the types of products and/or services the company will provide.

- Registered Agent—Virtually all states require corporations to have a registered agent in the state of formation. The registered agent is the party responsible for the receipt of important legal and tax documents for the corporation. The registered agent must have a physical address (no P.O. boxes) in the state of formation and must be available during normal business hours.

Examples of documents sent to the registered agent include Service of Process (or notice of litigation), which is the document that initiates a lawsuit; mail from the state; and often taxation documentation from the state's department of taxation.

The registered agent's address is a matter of public record. In states that do not require the legal address of the business to be included in the formation documents, the registered agent's address is the only address on file for the company. Many business owners, particularly home-based businesses, choose to use a registered agent provider both to ensure these important documents are professionally handled and to keep their addresses out of the hands of marketers.

- **Incorporator**—The incorporator is the person or company preparing and filing the formation documents with the state. Most states require the name and signature of the incorporator to be included in the formation documents and some also require the incorporator's address be included.

- **Number of Authorized Shares of Stock**—Corporations must outline the number of shares of stock they wish to authorize. While many people think only public companies have shares of stock, the reality is that all corporations, no matter how small, have stock. Stock represents the ownership in a corporation. As you consider how many shares of stock to authorize, keep in mind that a corporation does not need to issue the total number of authorized shares. Some corporations opt to hold a certain number of un-issued shares in order to add additional owners at a later date or to increase the ownership percentage for a current shareholder.

- **Share Par Value**—The par value of a share is its minimum stated value. Par value typically doesn't correlate to the actual value of a share. Common par values are $0.01, $1.00 or no par. The actual value of a share is its fair market value, or what someone is willing to pay for a share of stock. For public companies, actual value is determined by the price investors are willing to pay for each share on a national exchange. For private companies, the actual value of a share is typically determined by the overall value of the corporation or the book value.

- **Preferred Shares**—If a corporation plans to authorize both common and preferred shares, this information along with any information on voting rights must be included in the articles of incorporation. Preferred shares typically provide those shareholders with preferential payments of dividends or distribution of assets should the company cease operations. Many small business owners choose to only authorize shares of common stock. For additional information on preferred shares and voting rights it is best to seek the advice of an attorney.

- **Directors**—Many states require the names and addresses of the initial directors of the corporation to be included on the formation documents. The directors are the individuals responsible for overseeing and directing the affairs of the corporation, including making major corporate decisions. They are not responsible for the day-to-day activities of the business, which are the responsibility of a corporation's officers. Directors are elected by the shareholders and are also responsible for appointing the officers.

- **Officers**—While inclusion of the officer information is optional in many states, a few states do require it. The officers are responsible for the day-to-day activities of the corporation. Common officer titles include president, vice president, secretary and treasurer.

- **Legal Address of the Company**—Supplying the legal address, or the principal address, of the business is optional in many states but a few states do require it.

While this is not a complete list of everything a state might require on its articles of incorporation, it outlines the typical items and will help you assemble this information prior to starting the incorporation process.

COMPLIANCE REQUIREMENTS AND CONSEQUENCES

After the initial step of formation, both corporations and LLCs face ongoing compliance requirements; however, business owners, especially small business owners, often neglect these requirements. Whether the excuse is not knowing about them or not having time to address them, not satisfying these requirements is a big mistake.

Failing to complete ongoing requirements regularly and in a timely manner can have dire consequences. A company can lose its corporate or LLC entity status, and consequently lose the limited liability protection it affords the owners. Given that limited liability protection is often the primary reason business owners form a corporation or LLC, an owner should take all the necessary steps to protect it and the other benefits corporations and LLCs afford.

The Requirements

The requirements can be grouped into two categories: internal and external. Internal requirements are actions that must be taken within the corporation or LLC by the directors and shareholders or members and managers respectively. These actions must be documented and those documents kept with the company records. External requirements are those imposed on corporations and LLCs by the state in which they are formed or foreign qualified. These requirements often include an annual state filing and payment of a corresponding state fee.

Internal requirements are those most commonly overlooked. A corporation has the strictest internal requirements, including holding initial and annual meetings of directors and shareholders, adopting and maintaining updated bylaws, issuing stock to shareholders, and recording any subsequent stock transfers. While for an LLC it is not required, it is still recommended to adopt and maintain an updated operating agreement, issue membership shares, record any subsequent interest transfers, and to hold annual meetings of the members or managers.

Many business owners use a corporate kit or LLC kit for organizing records. These kits include items such as sample bylaws or an operating agreement, stock or membership interest certificates and transfer ledger, a corporate or LLC seal, and sample meeting minutes.

For external requirements, most states require corporations and LLCs to file an annual statement or annual report. Annual statements allow states to keep updated information on corporations and LLCs formed or qualified there. Because certain information included in the articles of incorporation or articles of organization does not require an amendment to update, such as the names and addresses of the directors of a corporation or the members or managers of an LLC, the states rely on updated information in the annual statement.

While most states require annual statements, some states require a biennial statement. In either case, the states typically require a fee be paid when these statements are returned to the state. These fees vary by state and often by entity type and can range from under $10.00 up to over $300.00.

Some states also have a franchise tax, which is essentially a fee paid to the state for the mere privilege of operating as a corporation or LLC formed or qualified in that state. The states employ different formulas for calculating the franchise tax. For example, the tax may be based on the corporation's or LLC's revenue or a corporation's number of authorized shares and par value.

The due dates for annual statements and franchise taxes vary by state. Some states connect these due dates to the anniversary of the corporation's or LLC's formation or qualification. Other states set a particular due date for all corporation annual statements and another for all LLCs. Because the annual statements and franchise taxes represent ongoing requirements corporations and LLCs will face, it is advisable for business owners to research these requirements prior to incorporating, so that they know what to expect going forward, and can attempt to budget for the cost.

In the entertainment business LLCs are often used when several individuals are going into business together as a production company or as studio owners. When you have a partnership, it is like a marriage so there must be trust and full disclosure at all times. Many projects today are not network or record company generated. They are privately funded. For that reason, many producers and artists maintain an LLC contracting company identity. They operate under that so they can do business across all the aspects of flow that their career creates.

THE CONSEQUENCES

If a corporation or LLC is sued and unable to show it indeed has met all of the corporate or LLC formalities and state requirements, a judge can rule that the company has been acting more like a sole proprietorship or general partnership. This can result in what is called "piercing the corporate veil." When the corporate or LLC veil is pierced, the limited liability protection of the entity disappears and the assets of the individual owner(s) are now accessible should a lawsuit judgment be made against the company.

There are also consequences on the state level that can happen prior to piercing the corporate veil. When a corporation or LLC does not comply with a state's annual or ongoing requirements, the company is no longer in "good standing" with the state.

Each state has different parameters for what is required before a company falls out of good standing and also how the states handle it. For example, many states impose late fees and interest payments on the outstanding annual statement and/or franchise tax fees.

Being out of good standing long enough may lead to administrative dissolution by the state. When the state administratively dissolves a corporation or LLC, all of the benefits of being a corporation or LLC are lost. In these instances, companies must be reinstated.

COMPLIANCE ASSISTANCE

There are a number of tools available today, such as online compliance management tools, many specifically geared towards small business owners, to help make the process of complying with both internal formalities as easy and convenient as possible. If you took the time to form your business as a corporation or LLC, you should also take the time to ensure it stays compliant and keeps its valued entity status.

This information appears courtesy of www.bizfilings.com. If you would like to have help forming your corporation, the experts there can help you through the whole process.

THE ACTUAL INCORPORATION PROCESS

Choosing a corporate name

A corporate identifier is a part of the entity name, such as "incorporated," "corporation," "company", "LLC", "ltd," "limited" or an acceptable abbreviation of these. The name can't be the same or too similar to an already incorporated business within the same state. It also can't attempt to capitalize on the reputation or identity of another registered business. If you decide to trademark your name, you can use it in all fifty states.

You might want to use some key words that will explain quickly what you do; such as productions, engineering, or entertainment. However, the corporate name can't imply affiliation with a religious, charitable, veteran, or professional organization without that tie being officially certified in writing. It can't be misleading—like you can't put, "bank" in your corporate name if the company has not satisfied state requirements for incorporating as a bank.

Have one or two other names chosen in case your first choice in name is taken.

Check the availability of the name choice

The name you choose for your business needs to be checked with the state you are incorporating with before you file your articles of incorporation. If you file any documents with a name that has already been taken, the filing will be rejected. To check availability, you can use name checks by phone, if available, or check your state's Website and perform a public records search online.

File the required documents

The documents that you must file in order to incorporate are known as the "articles of incorporation", "articles of organization", "charter" or "certificate of incorporation"— depending on your state. The articles are filed with your secretary of state office, or other business regulatory agency. Some states require that the articles of incorporation be filed with another informational form. Go to your state's Website to find out where to pick up and send in these documents. At that Website you will find the fees associated with filing and phone numbers of who you can call for questions.

Pay state filing fees

After those steps, you will need to follow up with these actions:

- Electing tax status with the IRS (remain a C corp. or file as a S corp.)
- Obtaining an employer identification number
- Opening a bank account
- Starting a corporate record book
- Domain name registrations

While these explanations seem drawn out and boring, it is part of the necessary dialog if you truly want to see your career of audio engineering take on more than just a work-for-hire experience. Make use of the Websites provided and do more research on your own to decide which plan is best for you. Author Marsha Sinetar penned a famous book called *Do What You Love: The Money Will Follow*. The information I am sharing with you allows you to set up your business correctly so that your money stays after it follows.

13

Setting Up
Long Money Situations

LITTLE MONEY IS MONEY TOO

If you have the opportunity to get points for engineering—great! If you have the knack for producing, and you get royalty points—great! But, if you are doing work for hire like many of us, then please consider focusing on the entry level of a long-money plan:

ALWAYS INVEST A PORTION OF YOUR EARNINGS. HERE ARE SOME SUGGESTIONS:

- Automatically put 10 percent of your earnings into savings (there are many high-yielding savings accounts that you can find by comparing different banks' rates online. Many times this money is easily accessible but at least it is making money for you.

- Get an IRA (Individual Retirement Account). Yearly contribution is usually maxed out at $4,000. If you are self-employed, SEP IRAs have a higher yearly contribution allowance ($14,000). The monies contributed to these accounts are tax deductible for that year. When you access the funds at retirement there might be tax implications. Please research which one is best for you and find the highest yielding one so it can accrue as much interest as possible.

- Do this every time you get a paycheck! Do this every time you get a paycheck! When you get into the habit of putting money away consistently, you will gain confidence knowing that you have something to fall back on if you have a slow work period. Getting a big paycheck is not always an opportunity to make big purchases.

- Set monetary goals for yourself in areas of savings, retirement accounts, and other investment accounts. Keep track of all the interest activity on your accounts at least four times a year. Interest rates change all the time and you want to make sure you are getting the best return on your money.

- As an independent, you have to look at every purchase. If it is not a necessity you need to ask, "Will this make money for me?" If the answer is yes, you can probably justify it as a company write off. If the answer is no, then you have to think not just twice but five times before you lay down that money!

  If you have a steady nine-to-five gig you cannot rely on that alone. If anything, you have even more of a responsibility to put money away every pay period!

- Live within or below your means while you are starting your long-term investment plan. As I said earlier, "Knowing how much it costs you to live on earth each day is crucial to the success of your basic plan."

- Research and invest in different types of funds that you can deal with yourself. Some examples would be accounts with companies like Charles Schwab, Fidelity, and Vanguard.

Although you hear about keeping your credit score high and credit report clean all the time, it really can make all the difference in the world. Until your business establishes its own credit, decisions are made based on yours. It can make or break your chances to get things like business loans, business credit cards, and the lowest possible interest rates.

INSURE

Understand the need for business and health insurance. When you are the company and you get sick, the office closes. Have a plan for coverage so that your business can run smoothly if you need to be somewhere else (family emergency, etc.). Remember to insure your equipment no matter where it is used. It is possible to insure your gear and have a policy that covers it when the gear is moved to different studios. Here are two providers that are experienced in insurance needs for entertainment situations. The firm of Robertson Taylor is also one of the largest insurance brokers that specialize in custom policies for all kinds of entertainment situations. I recently spoke with Keli Tomack, the vice president of the entertainment division, and she told me that they can create policies to cover individuals as well as companies and equipment (email: keli.tomack@rtib. net). For insurance specifically for recording studios and audio equipment, contact Joe Montarello (joem@capregins.com).

Get life insurance so that your family will be provided for in case you die. If you have children look into setting up a UGMA (Uniform Gift to Minor Account) or Education IRA.

Overall, having the financial aspect of the business figured out beforehand helps you work in all kinds of situations for any length of time. The money that you earn and invest lets you control your decisions without the normal pressures of the employer/employee relationship. I have seen many situations where the payment plan, when set up correctly, promotes better focus on the work (keep in mind those clients I spoke of who change personalities when money changes hands).

This is a condensed version of advice. By creating a basic system of simple things you always do when you handle your money, you can set yourself up for success in a relatively short amount of time.

As an independent contractor in the entertainment business, money comes in waves. Both small and large money situations help you achieve your immediate and long-term goals. I always use large projects to help me pay down on my overall debt and to invest for the future. By the way, investing doesn't always mean using money. I invest my time as well to help individuals as well as charity organizations. That's part of your responsibility to your community. While many might think that it sounds corny to "pay it forward," it is necessary to develop a way to tithe. Even if you are not a religious person, the "law of reciprocity" is a very active component to any successful career.

14

Visualization

MAKING YOUR OWN REALITY

Having worked with many artists, I always stop to ask them one question. "Did you imagine yourself doing what you do?" Most often the answer without hesitation is, yes! In some cases they would begin to tell me their story about how they used visualization for years.

At this point, I should say that there is a fine line between having a vision and having blinders on. Sometimes you are so wrapped up in the vision that you cannot see the reality around you. I always remind people that Hitler had a vision too, so be careful—it is nothing to be taken lightly!

The simplest way to explain what visualization is would be to think about where you see yourself in your career. Now, close your eyes and put yourself in the scene in your head. At the same time feel how happy that scene makes you feel. That is visualization. The religious world tells us "as a man thinketh, so shall he be." Webster's defines visualization as "to form a mental image."

The mind has the incredible power to alter your actions and attitude. A committed vision can change how you are, which can eventually change where you are. We have all heard of visualization used to help lose weight, stop smoking, improve golf swings, and much more. What I am talking about is using this ability to create a mental image of something as simple as a job completed on time.

Using visualization can actually help you think clearer when you are working with others. To help you make the correct choices when trying to communicate your ideas, keep a pad by your bed and write down all your thoughts, ideas, dreams, and goals. Cut pictures out and create a board that has imagery on it. Use it to help you focus. This is a popular technique taken directly from the movie and book by Rhonda Byrne, *The Secret*.

If what I am saying sounds strange, then try the following. Before you get up take about thirty seconds to imagine your day before you rise from your bed to meet the world. You will find that the time you take to prepare your mental images will have an instant effect on the flow of your day.

As an engineer, having a clear mind open to focus on the creative content of others is probably one of the strongest tools you have. Next time you get ready for a session visualize the steps that you will go through to set up and be prepared for the best possible session.

As I get older, I really use visualization to help me stop the rush of the day and take time for me. I create a mental image of me alive and healthy playing with my wife and kids. This image causes me to dedicate at least forty-five minutes each day to some kind of aerobic activity. Over the years, I have discovered that my health is just as important as my achievements in my profession.

I also imagine and visualize that my ideas and creative concepts are original and unique. My wife and I visualize our business activity, meetings, household goals, etc. We use visualization along with our faith to help set our mental state for achievement. I also use music. The introduction of the iPod has allowed me to take the music of my youth with me when I am thinking about mental images that relax me. When I am on studio projects I play music that is lyrically in line with what I am trying to do. Earth Wind & Fire does it every time when I want to be productive.

As I write this chapter, I am searching my memory banks for a good story of visualization. The rebuild of Paisley Park comes to mind. As I began touring the complex, I kept asking about all the different rooms and what they were used for. When I opened one particular door I found that it was a closet, which at one time doubled as a projection room. It was small but in my mind I got a picture, probably because I had been doing a lot of smaller creative spaces. I quickly scribbled a picture down and continued on touring the facility.

We soon got to work and after about three weeks of repairs we awaited the studio's famous owner to return to review the first phase of our work efforts. I had one week before the owner returned and I had a vision for that unused space and some extra materials. I quickly pulled out the picture I had sketched and began to draw some plans. We stripped the room, made all the changes, ran wires and had a full functioning studio complete with analog and digital tie lines to all of the other rooms in the facility as well as the sound stage.

Visualization helped me see in my mind what had to be done. We gathered all the materials and started to construct the room from the notes. The room came together and was completed on time and given the name "Studio D." Everyone on the engineering team worked off that one drawing and our knowledge of engineering and audio principles.

Upon his return, he toured the original repair and update work to studios A and B. He was very surprised to find a complete studio where a closet had been. After he left he instructed someone to let me know that he liked what I had done.

After that, we continued to convert many more closets into lounges and multi-media rooms. My goal was to create rooms that could be used for a multitude of purposes. There was no need to have unnecessary closets in a facility that is meant to serve creative people. I wanted to make every space efficient and able to make money.

In the end, we added a video edit suite, a studio lounge, two additional small production studios, a library, wardrobe shop, art department, automated conference room, and a hair salon. When I think back, my vision for Paisley Park Studios was that it could be a place where any artist could step in and fully conceptualize their creative ideas without restriction. I wanted to see everything in the facility working at one time problem-free. This had been the desire of the owner since its construction.

I took on that project because throughout my career I had been put in some very special settings that were almost always designed for me to do my very best. That was no different. Working with someone and being technically responsible for their creative environment is "major" as my friend George Shaw would say.

I knew that, just like my work with Herbie Hancock, the work I did (and continue to do) with Prince would have historic implications and be a set up for more music for years to come. In addition, I learned a lot about myself, in particular how much a technical person like me used artistic visualization to achieve my solutions.

When I watched the 2007 Golden Globe Awards, they announced the winner for best motion picture soundtrack. The winner was Prince for the title theme to the movie *Happy Feet*. The song was created in Studio D, the same closet at Paisley Park Studios! A vision in consort with just one committed individual can affect the world . . . and a closet as well.

Here is another example of how visualization in a group setting can be very powerful. In 2001, Darrell Diaz and I helped prepare an AES (Audio Engineering Society) keynote presentation for Herbie Hancock. We had visualized Herbie being able to play his remote keyboard in surround while delivering his keynote on the future of technology in our industry. As usual, Darrell prepped the software and I handled the hardware. The three of us had thought about it, discussed it, put it on paper and then assembled it. We were getting software updates right up until Herbie hit the stage.

He did the keynote address, put on his wireless remote keyboard, and began to play a lead line over a track of music. As he played, the lead sound whirled around the room. The three of us had visualized and prepared all that time for a moment that lasted less than thirty seconds. After that, the stage was set! We were now set to do the unthinkable and perform in surround with the ability to actively move every instrument in the surround field in real time. You see we knew that when we succeeded, the next challenge would be to do an entire band. We had already visualized the tour that was to come.

In 2002, we completed working on a studio project with Herbie Hancock called "Future2Future." It was an electronic project done in conjunction with Bill Laswell, the producer Herbie worked with on "Rock-it." We began to discuss the live tour. Herbie, Darrell, and I all wanted to do something different. We started to discuss what happened the last time they took an electric band out. I asked, "What were the biggest drawbacks?" The answer in unison was, "All that equipment!"

We soon decided to do the tour entirely from Apple laptops. The other two major components to our show were the use of visuals and our new presentation of the show in surround sound. Live surround sound had been done before, but it had always been presented in a similar fashion: four speakers in each corner of the venue all mixed by one engineer. At times that meant a lot of sound and no fluid movement. All the same source material came from each point and no speaker placement conformed to the venue size.

We had been using Pro Tools in the studio and been experimenting with expansion chassis and pushing our Mix Plus system to see how well it functioned when driven by a laptop. We had thought about the laptop as stage equipment long before it was the norm. For a jazz act to do an electric tour was not easy, even for someone as established as Herbie. The dollars are not always there to support the transportation of large amounts of gear.

Darrell and I worked on the software and hardware challenges. Herbie let us do our thing and stepped in to add the voice of experience. Herbie has always been known for ushering in the "new."

We contacted manufacturers and asked them questions like, "Can we use your product in a different way?" Most of the time the answer was, "We never really thought about that!" Answers like that and the ever popular, "It can't be done" were exactly why we proceeded forward. Always listen to the expert, because they can be wrong too.

To make a long story short, we took the concepts visualized in late-night meetings and created a way to do them. We toured for almost a year doing our version of "Live Surround." What made our version different is that we used two engineers and two separate sound systems. There was a normal stereo mixed show and a surround mix that was provided by the second engineer. We did this because we used sounds that were in motion real time as opposed to fixed position. We also left the placement of these sounds up to the engineer, making the surround mixer an actual member of the group. We placed our points to conform to the design of the venue. Each venue was different and each performance was special.

At the conclusion of our tour, Herbie and I visited the Digidesign headquarters and shared some of our notes with them. Several years later we were invited to a demo of a product called "Pro Tools Live" Or "Venue." Our visualization of doing something different combined with mutual commitment to a great show is what allowed us to take our studio tools and adapt them to solve our live needs. My hat is off to Herbie for trying our ideas out on the stages of the world.

I share this story with you not to say that Digidesign's Venue would not have existed without our efforts, but so that you will understand that the power of visualization when used in a group setting can produce results that no one ever imagined. Group visualization is just as important as individual visualization. When everyone is focused and in agreement, the result is dynamic.

Today, I use visualization in every aspect of my life. I did not realize it but I had been using it for years when I was in school as well as when I was working with my clients. Mixing is actually a good example of real time visualization. Engineers take the pieces of the acoustic puzzle they are given and they use their skills and experience to visualize an outcome or final mix.

I think that is why the talents of engineers are taken for granted many times. One of the most powerful things that everyone should learn about visualization is that it is not just a work tool, it is a life tool. When used in combination with your faith and individual belief systems it can propel you through anything. Each time you use it with intent and then see the results, you will understand how much you as an individual really add to every situation.

In the first story, the use of visualization to build a room that helped create a song that won an award, was for no other reason than this story. That is right. I built that room to tell this story. It was the committed vision that responded to me and gave me the opportunity to share it with you. One of my goals is to be able to help more people realize their individual importance in our world, and that one person can make a difference. So, by reading these words you are actually helping me achieve one of my goals! On my desk is a paperweight that has the words of Gandhi. It says, "Be the change you wish to see in the world." Visualization helps you see the world with the changes you wished for.

To see pictures of the studio discussed in this chapter go to: (www.PaisleyParkStudios.net).

To read more about Herbie Hancock's Future2Future Live go to: (www.futurestyle.org/arch#1CE7AA).

15

Business
Survival Stories

Folks, sometimes you have to laugh to keep from crying!
As you can see by now many things happen in this business. I have heard many say, "What doesn't kill you, makes
you stronger." If you can survive in this business at any
level, you are strong. Here are some of my thoughts and a
few more stories about folks "just doing business."

THE NEW BUSINESS MODEL

You Don't Want the Truth . . . You Can't Handle the Truth!

Well, for the last couple of years I have been listening to everyone rant about "The new business model of music." Here is my solution. Institute a mandatory rotation so no one gets comfortable. This means that everyone has to show results from day one. With record company folks on a two-year rotation and lawyers on a one-year rotation it removes the time for alliances and monopolies to develop. Everyone has to do their best as soon as possible so that they prove their worth.

Time is always on the side of those who hold the money. Let's switch that around and make the playing field truly equal. We all know what happens when one of the majors rejects a song submitted for an album by an artist, so now the artist can reject any executive that gives an unacceptable work effort!

Many of those involved in the industry "go along to get along." Instead, I say reward everyone based on what they have done in "sweat equity." Then the business model will truly be "new" without any of the old guard, only the select can play, elitist games that still go on today.

Corporate structures should still be competitive environments. With new blood comes new ideas and new money. For those of us who have been in the business for over ten years, we built our careers on work. Many people today show up and do not want to put in the time or the work to be able to handle the position they seek with responsibility.

Let's get real simple. The music business still needs to be about the music! If you didn't write the tune then you are part of the support cast. It's called supply chain economics. If you aren't making the product then you are possibly touching it while it's in motion to the marketplace. It's real easy to see that even if a product cannot be controlled, and its flow into the marketplace can, the flow becomes more powerful that the product ever could.

I wrote this short piece called "Remember" after hearing a songwriter tell me a story about how they had gotten a chance to work with a heavyweight producer. Upon entering the studio he was told by the producer, "I don't care what you think needs to happen on your song, if it comes in this door I am going to put strings on it and we are going to split writers credit down the middle." As I was told the story all I could envision was that famous producer standing in the studio complete with peg leg, parrot, and eye patch. This is what takes place every day, and this for lack of a better term is called "business."

Remember that great song you wrote? Everyone thought it was great and you even played it for a couple of established artists who said they would like to use it.

Remember that great song you co-wrote? After you decided to work with one of these famous folks you were assigned a writing partner and your idea was then officially a part of the hit-making machine. You finally learned the meaning of the expression "going along to get along."

Remember that song? When you finally got through your turn around the track called "musical funding" you owned less than one-half of your original idea. But you managed to make a host of new friends who were all assigned to your new level of popularity and who all generated dollars off of the production of your song. You learned how much it costs you to be big time. **You do remember the song, don't you?**

Having worked in many camps I have had a front row seat to witness all the angels and devils at work side by side. I have an expression that goes like this, "Kling-ons don't just exist on a television show!" They are alive and well in the entertainment business. Doesn't matter what you call them, they all look and act the same.

They travel close by the artist at all times and never really do any skilled labor function. They complain constantly about conditions or everyone else's incompetence. Kling-ons usually drink and smoke way too much, and are basically just skating by being in orbit around someone famous. Many of them are life long friends. Many are just office workers too comfortable to remember that in the end they are not the one going on stage to perform every night.

Whatever the case, our business is changing so fast many Kling-ons are about to get left behind. I for one will be happy when some of the Kling-ons wake up and realize that they could do more good for themselves and others just by raising the level of their individual game. Here's an example:

I once knew an engineer who was very skilled. The only drawback was that he had to smoke a joint every day and he had no goals other than working and scoring more dope. This guy had worked with everybody, yet carried himself as if he were homeless. Many times I would listen to his stories and tell him, "Man you are a walking history of certain events!" All he would do was take a long draw from his joint and say, "Man that's not me."

Meanwhile we all were getting older. Pretty soon he started to realize that there was a new kind of engineer available. One who went to school and intended on doing exactly what they were doing, and didn't need to smoke a joint every day. But it was too late. This guy had worked for thirty-plus years on the "all I need is a joint in the morning principle." He smoked his best self away. I tell you about him not only as a message about the perils of drugs, but also as a lesson about wasting time on low expectations.

Here is another example of not so much failure, but a low aim. I know a famous entertainer who has a small camp of people. Now because he acts in movies his assistant, manager, and attorney keep track of his activities daily. When I was asked to work with him, I was there in a music capacity by direct invitation of the artist. That caused strife in the beginning because the handlers wanted to know who I was and why did I have direct access. To an outsider like me it seemed almost as if they were trying to control the flow of individuals around him.

Anyway, as we worked they eventually were responsible for supporting the artist's musical endeavors too. One day I asked the personal assistant who worked with him, "What's the tension I feel every time these people come in the studio?" I was shocked at the response. The attorney, the manager, and the business assistant all thought that it was useless for the artist to do music. They felt that he made more money under contract doing movies so they tried not to encourage what he wanted to do in music. They also did their best to show the endeavor as a financial loss so that it became a business decision rather than support something that their client wanted to do.

While reflecting on that experience, I remember a valuable lesson I learned from Herbie Hancock. It was to basically always give him the opportunity to choose what he wanted to do. Even though he might have me on board for my knowledge in a certain area, I respected the fact that the final choice was his. As an engineer, this one piece of information has made a big difference for many of my clients.

I see different situations all the time where creative options are ushered out of the room by business. That has more to do with what's best for the handlers rather than what's best for the artist who is paying everyone by creating the art that they peddle.

One thing the "joint-smoking" engineer from the previous story and the handlers from this story had in common was to act as though each entertainer they worked for would not have been successful without their services. It's funny and it's sad. How many times have we all seen engineers, attorneys, managers, and assistants stand in the wings and act as though they were the talent that the audience bought tickets to see. It's this high level of arrogance that fuels entertainers to find the most joy when they are with their instrument rather than with the people around them that glean a living from their existence. Comedian Dave Chappelle said, "When you make a lot of money and are successful, people have a vested interest in trying to control you."

I guess what I would really like to see from everyone is a higher level of service in our industry. By providing good service and supporting every artist who hires your services the work will come. There's no need to invent new ways to exploit and subvert the work processes related to content creation. There is enough work for everyone, so take your time and remember it is a service-oriented business! Around the corner we all must learn how to move forward and be as strong about our creativity both individually and collectively as we are about securing the dollars that are associated with the world of electronic content.

For us to survive as an industry we have to have a safe middle ground for all to operate. Having a pre-negotiated meeting point will help to open the doors and get more than just one person's creative viewpoint. It's a great song that starts it all. Mix that with a producer's vision and the sweat equity of great engineers and musicians and you once again have a prosperous circle of activity that feeds many households and in turn promotes creative people to actually want to work together again.

While I understand that clique-like tribal activity will always exist, it is necessary to look at how our industry has evolved in a very short amount of time from being song driven to being spin driven. Quality, trust, and talent have to matter for dynamic change to occur in anyone's life—let alone our industry. So before we go searching all over for the elusive "new business model," I think we all could use an upgrade on ourselves. In the end, this business wouldn't be a business without the people.

REAL JOBS GET REAL CHECKS!

I recently did a job that enlisted the help of some of my friends. Or, so I thought. For some time, I had been wondering how valuable I was as a resource to those around me in my profession. In simple terms, I wanted to know whether I had spread the wealth or if I was stingy. I was once told, "You know you are doing well when your friends are doing well." So, I sat down and looked at my record keeping books to find out if I had been hitting my goals. One of my goals was that everyone around me was to be doing well. I found that indeed I had reached and even surpassed my goals.

I also found that in some cases I had one-way friendships. I had given many opportunities to others, but received no referrals or calls when they needed a service I could provide. I share this with you to set the stage for the following lesson.

I had asked a tech friend of mine Denny, whom I had known for twelve years to do some wiring and tech work on this job. I let him make his own fees and even fly in and out to complete his work so he could still have family time. Over the years, I had turned over many large jobs to him that totaled well over $50,000 in work.

This job was especially rough. We had to work during periods where there were full sessions going on. Sometimes during the down time I would gather everyone in a room to discuss the operational goals while we were in session. As we were meeting one day, the subject of a new small mastering room came up. It was my job to design and implement any projects of this nature.

Denny made an interesting comment that stuck with all of us until this day. He started to speak about how he thought the room could be designed. "Well, in a real studio, this is what happens," he said.

All of us paused, looked at him but said nothing. At that moment, I realized that our twelve years together meant nothing to him. My calls and referrals for him to do other work meant nothing. In his mind, this job was not real.

He started to correct himself and said, "Well, you know when (drop a name studio design firm) does it, they do this. And it has to be this way or it's not professional."

I listened and ended the meeting. Later that afternoon I spoke to him alone about it. I asked him one simple question: When you send in a real invoice does it get paid with real money? When he said nothing, I let him know that at any time he felt that this job wasn't real he should give back the money and not do the job. He knew he was wrong but was too proud to admit it.

Here is my point: our business is one where you determine what is real by how serious you take your work. Just because the books and magazines are filled with faces that might not look like you or me doesn't mean that the work that you are doing is not real. Careers are made up of years of using your skills over and over. My career has allowed me to use my engineering and technical skills in many environments. If I said, "I am only going to work on records," I would not have worked at all in many cases. My first attempts at designing production rooms and studios led to the larger work I now do. While the path I took might not be like the one taken by the other designers or engineers, it is just as real.

The same holds true for your career. What Denny didn't realize was that I am in a position to offer him employment because I started out doing every job that I now contract to others. It is okay to have a big vision for your career. However, not everyone (sometimes not even your friends) will share in your big vision. Denny did not have a bigger vision for himself; therefore, he could not share in a bigger vision for others.

I'm thankful that Denny showed us who he truly was. By his words and his actions he actually made it clear to me and to the world what kind of person he truly is deep down. Does clarity count for anything? No. Is there a line for clarity at the bank? No. However, there is now a space in my database for a new technician!

JUST BECAUSE IT'S QUIET DOESN'T MEAN NOTHING IS GOING ON!

When I first started as an independent, I tried many ways of doing business. The simple way was and still is a DBA. While my audio modifications and tech service was fine, I also did some small audio installations. I was just beginning to do more home studio design and installations when I was asked by a friend to form a company to do some installs and light studio stuff. His trade skill was in cabinet design. While I did do studios, I did not always have a need for a cabinet maker.

I tried a DBA partnership. I knew that I had much more experience than my friend who had asked to be partners. I decided to let him lead since he was so interested in working together. I thought by giving him an opportunity to control the books he could get the vision that I had seen when I started my career. I let him set up the business. I let him hold the checkbook. All I asked was that at tax time I didn't get any special stories—just to give my accountants the right reports and everything would be fine. I understood that I had several streams of income that made going into a limited partnership like this a calculated risk.

Isn't it interesting that most people tend to assume that quiet people are not watching every little detail? What I began to notice was that this fool actually thought that my other work was something that he needed to be part of. Somewhere he had assumed that my client list was his too. In addition, he seemed to feel that his audio and technical ability had leaped ahead of everyone around him. He also proved that he couldn't handle the leadership role in the business due to the fact that when tax time came my accountants never received the paperwork that was requested.

It turned out that he was doing so much in so many areas he was mixing his money together to survive. The whole time he was acting like everything was cool. He thought timid Dave was not paying attention. I asked three times for the documentation, and when I got no response I made my mind up to not do any type of business with him

EVER. I gave no explanation, I just walked away and told him to keep whatever money was not being revealed and I went on my way. Our account was closed and I severed ties between us.

I did not call him again and I did not slander him to our colleagues. I said nothing and moved forward toward my destiny. I chose not to expose the truth about him because I was moving forward. It would have been counterproductive because I always let my truth be established by the results of my work.

I learned several valuable lessons. One of which was the fact that just because it's your time doesn't mean that it's your friend's time as well. My efforts to work with him were because deep down I felt guilty about my career moving considerably faster than that of my peers.

The other lesson was that there is more power in saying NO than there is in saying YES. In many situations the seemingly more dominant person will feel that they are actually smarter than everyone else around. Pride and ego don't allow them to see what's really going on. My friend thought that because he held the checkbook, he held the power over me to produce a result for his benefit. He did not understand that my allowing him to hold a checkbook meant nothing other than me giving him an opportunity to grow. He also didn't realize that holding a checkbook is figurative power at best, literal power is what counts and I don't keep that in a checkbook.

As an audio professional your skills will start to open many doors, so be prepared. The ability to see the big picture at all times is what helps people get past the BS of business. Intent is what makes you operate in complete faith. The next time you are in a meeting, look for the person saying the least. Take time to study the room. If you are usually the one who talks then stay silent and listen; you might just learn something.

Resources

MAGAZINES

- *Mix* (www.mixonline.com)
- *Audio Media* (www.audiomedia.com)
- *Billboard* (www.billboard.com)
- *EQ* (www.eqmag.com)
- *Entertainment Design* (www.livedesignonline.com)
- *Electronic Musician* (www.emusician.com)
- *Live Sound International* (www.livesoundint.com)
- *Music Connection* (www.musicconnection.com)
- *Post* (www.postmagazine.com)
- *Recording* (www.recordingmag.com)

- *Remix* (www.remixmag.com)
- *Sound and Video Contractor* (www.svconline.com)
- *Sound on Sound* (www.soundonsound.com)
- *Tape OP* (www.tapeop.com)
- *The Hollywood Reporter* (www.hollywoodreporter.com)
- *Pro Sound News* (www.prosoundnews.com)
- *Surround Professional* (www.surroundpro.com)
- *Video Systems* (www.digitalcontentproducer.com)
- *Variety* (www.variety.com)

WEBSITES

- www.davehampton.com
- www.monstercable.com
- www.glyphtech.com
- www.hypnotic-audio-secrets.com
- www.dangerousmusic.com
- www.adam-audio.com
- www.audiographintlstore.com
- www.rackmountcity.com
- www.janalcase.com
- www.digidesign.com
- www.apple.com
- www.motu.com
- www.zproductguy.com
- www.rspe.com
- www.forat.com

- www.gcpro.com
- www.westlakeaudio.com
- www.state.gov/documents/organization/88661.pdf

CAREER WEBSITES

- www.about.salary.com
- www.payscale.com
- Applause Music Careers: www.cnvi.com/applause
- Entertainment Careers: www.entertainmentcareers.net
- Entertainment Jobs: www.entertainmentjobs.com
- Maslow Media Group: www.maslowmedia.com
- MIDI and Audio jobs: www.midi.org
- Showbiz Jobs: www.showbizjobs.com
- TV Jobs: www.tvjobs.com
- Vault: www.vault.com
- IATSE: www.iatse-intl.org
- LA411: www.la411.com
- Gig List: www.giglist.org
- Backstage jobs: www.backstageJobs.com
- Roadie Jobs: www.roadiejobs.com
- Roadie: www.roadie.net
- Roadie Show: www.roadieshow.com
- Rigger's Page: www.rigging.net
- Record Label Resource: www.recordlabelresource.com
- Audio Mastermind: www.audiomastermind.com (database)
- eSession: www.esessions.com

ORGANIZATIONS TO JOIN

- AES (www.aes.org)
- SPARS (www.spars.com)
- RIAA (www.riaa.com)
- IRTS (www.irts.org)
- AFM (www.afm.org)
- NARIP (www.narip.com)
- IATSE (www.iatse.org)
- SMPTE (www.smpte.org)
- NSCA (www.nsca.org)
- MPSE (www.mpse.org)
- NAPRS (www.naprs.org)
- NAB (www.nab.org)
- LAMN (www.lamn.com)
- GANG (www.audiogang.org)
- AFTRA (www.aftra.com)
- NARAS (www.naras.org)

BOOKS TO READ

The Bible

Who Moved My Cheese? by Spencer Johnson, M.D.

The Leadership Skills of Attila the Hun by Wess
Roberts, Ph.D.

Who's Afraid of a Large Black Man by Charles Barkley

Why Business People Speak Like Idiots by Fugere, Haraway & Warshawsky

Open Mike by Michael Eric Dyson

The Art of War / The Art of Small Business by Sun Tzu & Gary Gagliardi

Behold a Pale Horse by William Cooper

The 48 Laws of Power by Robert Greene

The Way of Go by Troy Anderson

The Richest Man in Babylon by George S. Clason

The Automatic Millionaire by David Bach

The Carrot Principle by Adrian Gostick and Chester Elton

About the Author

Dave Hampton
Audio Engineer Studio Designer Technician Author Educator

For over 25 years, Dave Hampton has contributed to the success of many artists. Among the most famous faces you will find such legendary artists as Babyface, Herbie Hancock, and Prince. Through his company MATK Corp, he specializes in dedicated support services for all entertainment-related activities. Whether it's consulting on a million-dollar recording facility or a personal home recording room, album project or live tour, Hampton's reputation is one of providing solutions and getting the job done. Trust and personal service are the core elements of his success.

Ever since the rising demand for home studios began, Dave has played a significant role in educating artists as to the capabilities of defining their own creative spaces. He has designed, built and modified studios and equipment for the likes of Herbie Hancock, Sinbad, Rafael Saadiq, Maxwell, and Organized Noyze. Dave's expertise allowed him to also design and build large-format studios for The Famous Radio Ranch, Creflo Dollar and World Changers

Ministries, Babyface, Marcus Miller, and he recently completed the restoration of Paisley Park Studios for Prince.

He has designed touring rigs for live concerts to include custom instrument modification for touring musicians like the band Chicago and solo artists Maxwell and Whitney Houston. He has been pivotal in the production and engineering of projects for Grammy-winning artists Herbie Hancock and Marcus Miller. In fact, in the year 2000, he was the first engineer on record to use Pro Tools to mix a live concert show when Herbie Hancock toured Europe and performed entirely in surround sound.

Recent positions Dave has held include Technical Director for both Prince at Paisley Park Studios in Minneapolis (three years) and for Herbie Hancock at Hancock Music (ten plus years) in Los Angeles. In addition, he serves on the steering committee for the Producers and Engineers Wing of the Recording Academy (NARAS) and is an active member of SPARS and AES. He currently works with many technology companies as an industry consultant and is on several audio education advisory boards.

Here is a partial list of Dave's clients:
- Babyface
- Bill Withers
- Charter Cable Studios
- Chicago
- Comedy Express TV

- Eddie Murphy
- First Avenue Night Club
- George Duke
- Happy Madison Productions
- Herbie Hancock
- Jeffery Osbourne
- Johnathan Butler
- Justin Timberlake
- Kenneth Crouch
- Kenny Lattimore
- Kirk Whalum
- Larry Graham
- Lincoln Memorial Church
- Marcus Miller
- Maxwell
- Organized Noyze
- Percy Bady
- Prince
- Raphael Saadiq
- Rutherford Sports Entertainment
- Shelia E.
- Sinbad
- Sir Gant
- The Crusaders
- Victory Bible Church
- Wayne Shorter
- Whitney Houston
- World Changers Ministries
- World Famous Radio Ranch